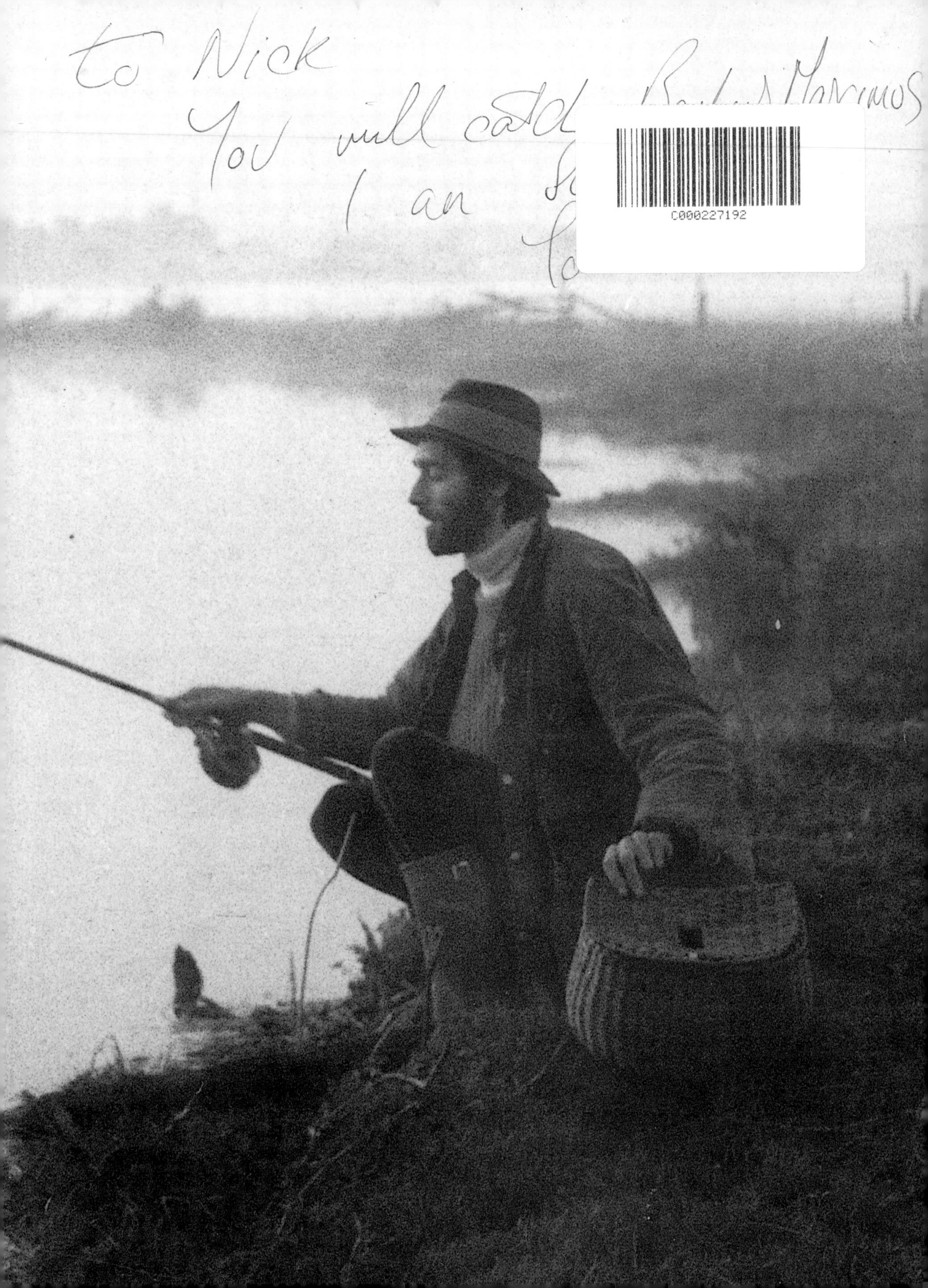
to Nick
You will catch Barbel Maximus
I am su
lo

The Deepening Pool

CHRIS YATES

The Deepening Pool

UNWIN HYMAN
LONDON SYDNEY WELLINGTON

First published in Great Britain by Unwin Hyman, an imprint of
Unwin Hyman Limited, 1990

Design by The Magill Design Company

UNWIN HYMAN LIMITED
15/17 Broadwick Street, London W1V 1FP

Allen & Unwin Australia Pty Ltd
8 Napier Street, North Sydney, NSW 2060, Australia

Allen & Unwin New Zealand Ltd with the Port Nicholson Press
Compusales Building, 75 Ghuznee Street, Wellington, New Zealand

British Library Cataloguing in Publication Data
Yates, Christopher
The Deepening Pool
1. Avon. Avon Valley. Angling freshwater
I. Title
799.1'1'094239

ISBN 0-04-440577-4

Typeset by Tradespools Ltd, Frome
Colour origination by Tenon & Polert Ltd, Hong Kong
Printed and bound by Butler & Tanner Ltd, Frome

To Clare, Camilla and Alexander,
and to the memory of
Donald F. Leney.

With my silken line and delicate hook
I wander in a myriad of ripples
And find freedom.
Li Yu, Fisherman's Song
(Tenth century, China)

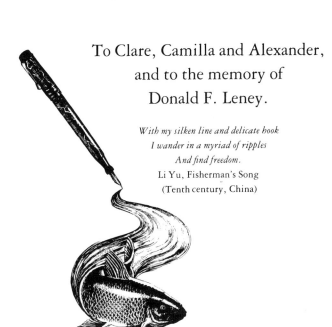

CONTENTS

ACKNOWLEDGEMENTS

I liked the thought of writing this book, yet were it not for the intervention and encouragement of others it would have remained nothing more than an idea.

Firstly I must thank Lesley Gowers, the editor of my first book, for introducing me to Merlin Unwin who subsequently encouraged me to write this, the second one. Being a fisherman himself makes Merlin not only a good editor of angling books, but also a very understanding one. However, he deserves a medal, juggling his schedules, shifting his deadlines and generally allowing me far too much freedom to 'search for inspiration' by the waterside.

Special thanks to my glorious wife, Gaffer. She decided that the only way to ensure that I finished this was to put me under house arrest. Non-one was allowed to visit me, phone calls were intercepted, my trousers were hidden from me. Yet while the Gaffer also shielded me from domestic travails and brought me breakfast in bed, she also had time to do me some exquisite illustrations for the chapter headings.

My good friend Shaun Alonso Hagen helped me copy out my original scrawl and make it legible to my superb typist Pat Taylor. When I began this book, Edward Barder, rod maker, supplied me with a very good bottle of ink and when I finished it, Nigel Parker Haywood supplied me with a very good bottle of port.

Thank you all very much.
Now for the moment of truth.

PREFACE

This book began almost by accident on the banks of the Hampshire Avon in the spring of 1989 and was completed exactly twelve months later. It follows a parallel course to my first book, *Casting at the Sun*, which describes my experiences on the ponds and lakes of Southern England. This book, however, is chiefly about moving waters, although there are several still water interludes.

Much of my boyhood was spent by streams and small rivers and, like the course of a stream, the following pages meander from those early days, when a pound chub was regarded as an improbable dream, to the present, where my zest for barbel fishing on the Hampshire Avon has superseded my quest for monster carp. Now my love for this river has forced me to desert all the waters I grew up with and a pound chub is almost regarded as an irritant.

But, while the locations and the objects of my angler's desire have changed, one thing remains constant: I still look upon living water with a child's vision; the deep pools of a river or the shadowy depths of a lake continue to excite my imagination and I remain fascinated and intoxicated by the thought of what might be down there.

The magic of water was the inspiration for this book and it is distressing that so much of that quality has been lost. Without life there can be no magic and since I was a boy too many beautiful rivers have been sacrificed to the greed of the intensive trout farmer, the profit motive of the agro-chemical industry or the ruthless efficiency of the water authorities.

However, though no fisherman can afford to ignore the threats to his world, this book is not about such life-sapping subjects. It is about the authentic adventure that an angler can still discover if he knows where to look and how to look.

Chris Yates

CHAPTER ONE

The View from
a Fishing Hut

*A river is water in its loveliest form; rivers have life and sound and movement and
infinity of variation, rivers are veins of the earth through which the life blood returns to
the heart.*
Roderick Haig-Brown . A River Never Sleeps (1948)

It is about noon on a mild day in early March. Heavy
clouds are piling up in the north and west, but at
the moment the sun is shining, a thrush is singing and
spring is surely here.

I am sitting in a salmon fishers' hut on the middle
Avon, with the river sliding by, bank-high and turbulent, just below the window. It bends sharply above
and below the hut, winding between water meadows, willow clumps and dense
osier beds. My cup of tea is steaming on the table, my rod is leaning against the
open door.

I can see my friend Jardine, way downstream, casting his Devon minnow
with slightly less fervour than was evident before. First thing this morning,
with the rising river looking as if it should be bulging with spring salmon, Jardine's casting was erratic. Now, when it seems as if Avon springers really are a
thing of the past, his casting is perfect. I have a nice old piece of Hardy cane (an
L.R.H. No. 1) and a pre-war Altex, and was looking forward to testing this
combination on a sprightly fish, but, having been flailing about since dawn, I
confess that my heart does not yearn for a silver tourist today.

To be successful in angling it must be absolutely necessary that you can catch

10

*I am sitting in a salmon fisher's hut with the river
sliding by just below the window.*

fish. You have to need your quarry, though if there are no fish in the river this desire will eventually lead to madness. This is one of the drawbacks of salmon fishing. However, if you are cunning you will regard a fish as a crass intruder and therefore savour every moment of your fishing, enjoying the river, the surroundings and your freedom, and happily not catch anything at all. Today I know I shall not catch anything. I may, I suppose, cast a few lines at sunset, but till then I shall spend my time watching the water, drinking tea and jotting. But first I shall have my lunch …

It is now about an hour into the afternoon – I can't be more precise because I do not possess a watch. Jardine has been, lunched and gone again, still hoping for a salmon, though his optimism is being menaced by reality. A great crested grebe has just surfaced in the quiet water under the far bank. He is looking in this direction, though I don't think he can see me. Now he has dived again, with a fluid downpouring of neck and body. Where will he surface? There, at least twenty yards upstream and out in the main current. There is no question of his need to catch fish, yet how can he see what to jab for in this coloured water?

Clouds have come in from the west and the river has darkened. It still shimmers where the current is deflected or interrupted by sudden changes of contour below; the smooth slow glide under the far bank looks black, while the fast water coming round the upstream bend flickers with light. Everything in the river is running at full power. The eddies are whirling, like great turbines; the weirs are thundering through the wide-open hatches; the long straights are like race tracks, dotted with speeding jetsam; last summer's reeds are all leaning over in the current, softly rattling and chafing; the bankside willows are knee-deep in the surge. I like to see it like this, especially as this is the first big push of water for weeks. On such a day I shouldn't be casting with vain hope for a non-existent salmon, I should be pitting my rods against something more realistic. Out of the force of the main current – and that quieter stretch under the far bank has just caught my eye again – I am sure I could find a big golden barbel. In fact if one showed itself now, rolling over on the surface as they sometimes do, I would certainly put down this pen and pick up my rod. But this is meant to be a salmon-fishing day and I have no barbel tackle or bait. Perhaps it's just as well. The wind has got up, it looks like rain and I think I might be breaking out into a new book. Where better to begin such a thing than in a fishing hut? But *how* to begin?

I suppose I should start with the Avon, a river that swept my heart away years ago. Nowadays I never feel completely happy with my fishing unless I'm casting into it. In fact, whenever I fish elsewhere, my thoughts are constantly returning here and I imagine what the water must be looking like at certain favourite pools and glides. I am an angler obsessed; the river has got into my veins.

This is all very strange, for though I have fished many different rivers since I was a boy my original angling home was amongst the carp pools of Surrey and Sussex. When I first fished the Avon I was living in a carp fisher's paradise near Haslemere and had just recently caught a record fish after twenty years of carp fishing. I suppose the time was ripe for a change of scene and species, yet this was not how I felt and I presumed, in fact, that I would continue being a merry carp fanatic until the end of my line. However, as I shall probably describe in detail later, I discovered the barbel; the barbel led me to the Avon; the Avon persuaded me to abandon my former obsession and now I live in a cottage on the Wiltshire–Dorset border, fifteen minutes from the river.

But even I do not want to live too close. It is a mistake to get too close to the water. The pleasures of returning are always keener if you have to travel a few miles first. I content myself with the knowledge that if I needed to be more permanently by the river I could always come and live in a salmon hut.

This has given me a new idea. There are dozens of salmon fishers' huts up and down the Avon and it would be rather nice to write each chapter in a different hut, even though many of them are dilapidated, some without even a roof. No, perhaps not. All right in the summer, but in weather like this, with no roof, the ink would run down the page and, to maintain body heat, I would probably drink too much brandy.

As I write, raindrops are speckling the window. The wind is even stronger than before and the willows are shuddering in the gusts. Where is Jardine? Has he got carried away by the current after being hauled in by a fish? I would have thought this storm would have driven him back for tea by now, but all I can see through the rain is a perky redshank and a forlorn-looking pony.

Though I did not cast my first line into the Avon until I was thirty-four, I think the reason it made such a subsequent impact on me was because the river had been running through my head since I was a boy. I saw it, just once, when I was ten and immediately thought it the most beautiful river in the world. I was travelling in the Yates family car, a 1936 Morris Eight, heading for a farmhouse holiday in Dorset. It was hot and I remember the car smelt strongly of orange peel and old leather. We stopped for some fresh air near a town that might have been Ringwood, or perhaps Fordingbridge. And there was the Avon, rippling towards us from between the water meadows. Of course the contrast to the car's stuffy interior helped to heighten the effect, but the river looked brighter and more exquisite than any I had seen before.

There was a luminous blue sheen over the surface and I could almost see a convex curve across the width of the river, so that it seemed near to overflowing. Seen from above, the water was as transparent as the finest glass. With a weird, contradictory slow motion, long streamers of vivid green weed swayed in the

Something fabulous was about to appear at any moment.

powerful current. Between the weedbeds the gravel shone golden, though just downstream was a darker place where it shelved steeply into a mysterious chasm. Down there, no doubt, shoals of fish lay hidden and, though I saw nothing, I expected something fabulous to materialize at any moment.

I could have happily stood on those banks for the rest of the holiday, yet, in spite of the impression the river made on me and the subsequent books and articles I read about it, which all confirmed that impression, twenty-four years went by before I saw the Avon again.

For a while the memory of it remained bright, but the family did not journey that way again and it was a hundred miles from home. By the time I was able to travel that kind of distance by myself I was more interested in discovering new carp ponds. The Avon began to flow underground, coming to the surface in dreams or at those odd times when I tired of static reflections and felt suddenly drawn to moving water again. I would fish the rivers near home and, though I often thought of travelling down to the Avon, I never did. Once or twice I almost went, after a string of happy days on some local stream inspired me with thoughts of something grander and more challenging. But then a friend would come and talk to me about carp, or I would recall a pond I had not visited for a while and which suddenly seemed unignorable. Then the Avon would seem far too far away and it would glide again into subconsciousness.

Yet, though I spent more and more time by still waters, moving water never lost its attraction. I was always pleased to spend the odd day watching a float weaving down the current, and it was a delight simply watching the river itself, surrounding myself with a single movement and letting my thoughts drift downstream. It all contributed to the general flow which suddenly broke surface with a wild enthusiasm when I first went down to the Avon with a rod.

The rain has stopped and the sky is now clearing, shot through with a single shaft of white light. Also, the wind has died back so that the river's surface is more glassy, enabling me to see again all the variations of current. I heard a kingfisher earlier then, later, saw him zip past the window, turn suddenly and arrow across the water. He had the iridescence and the flight pattern of a bluebottle. The redshanks have also been calling, occasionally filling the air with their clear, evocative chant, a sound I always associate with a river landscape in

spring.

Still no sign of Jardine, though it is about tea time. Should I worry about him and go in search of him or should I remember that time is elastic when you are fishing? What seems like an age to someone just sitting watching is but the briefest interval to a man fishing. Moreover, while a day fishing still water passes quickly, on a fast river it cannot be counted a day at all, more a blur. A good day's fishing will take twice as long to record in a diary than it did to live through, yet it never takes me more than an hour to write up even the most epic day. That is why I do not possess a watch. An angler cannot synchronize himself to such an artificial, inflexible measure of time as that dictated by the hour hand.

We exist in a different sort of time altogether. Yet life flies by too quickly even if you stare all day at a wall, which is why, according to my theory, all anglers are still children. Though they might live to be a hundred, they will never live long enough to grow up.

Ah! Here is Jardine, approaching along the bank with a toiling gait, as if he has been either struggling with a monster or trying unsuccessfully to paddle upstream in a bath-tub. Even as I write he comes, tackle-laden and heavy-footed, through the door, splashing drops of water across these soluble words (yet this old Swan is so much nicer than a Bic). Though he looks fatigued he surely has a story to tell and I shall set it down directly, letting his account break up this rambling text.

'Well,' I say, 'tell me what happened.'

'I got wet and cold and now all I want is a hot mug of tea.'

We sip our scalding beverage in near-silence. There have been, he says, no fish, no signs of fish, no approximations to fish, no imagined fish. Thus does the early spring salmon angler, who set out at sunrise with high heart, finally accept the futility of his dream. Yet if he had only brought some sensible tackle he could have shrugged off his fantasy and gone fishing for something real …

The clouds have lifted completely and the sun's reflections fill the hut with a hypnotic pulsating light. It took only this optimistic glow and a single cup of tea to restore shattered hopes and propel Jardine back into the watery fray. He now insists that his best chance will come at sunset. Thus does the early spring salmon angler never learn, though I admit that the river does look suddenly inviting and promising. Also, this high water is all the rage with the salmon fishers' textbooks. I shall have a last cast, then return to my theme, which I was just warming to. I shall probably remain here until midnight, for I have a stub of candle in my creel and a bottle of ink. I want to go back in time, for, while I have been writing, numerous half-forgotten rivers and streams have been coming back into focus, waters where I spent many happy days and where a course was set which would lead meanderingly, convolutedly, yet inevitably to this valley.

CHAPTER TWO

Monsters

Though still waters ran deepest, moving waters ran strongly enough through my childhood for me to become familiar with several different rivers and streams, most of which I either fished or fell into. I especially liked those quick clear streams where I could see down into the depths and watch for fish moving in the current. In fact, because most of my childhood streams ran clear, certainly much clearer and purer than they are now, I felt that this was their chief attraction. The ponds I fished were all wonderful places, but they were muddy or dark and you only saw a fish if it leapt clear of the surface. Ponds were full of unknown, invisible creatures, like an unillustrated book of mysteries. But streams and rivers were like books with pages full of colour and light. Along a riverbank you only had to be quiet and concentrate and a new world became visible, though, mostly, this was only the small, sparkling world of minnows, gudgeon and young dace. However, there was always the possibility of something grander and, very occasionally, I would be granted a sight that would almost topple me into the water.

I remember, on the Mole at Mickelham, climbing into a willow that hung over a shoal of fish all much larger than any I'd seen in a river before. They were chub and they were so close to the surface that I could almost have touched their olive-green backs with the toe of my boot.

Having previously spotted the fish, I'd crept along the bank and into the branches as carefully as a stalking cat. Yet once I was above the shoal, though I must have been visible to them, they were not disturbed by my presence, and chub are famous for their circumspection.

They seemed completely oblivious of me and it was marvellous to be able to study them in detail at such close proximity, especially as I'd only had a fleeting glimpse of a chub before. They were not at all like the fixed, unconvincing profiles in my book; this was the real thing, glorious, dynamic and vital. As I watched them holding their places in the strong current it seemed that their power and energy must be inexhaustible, limitless. Surely they must occasionally seek the quieter water, there to rest tired fins, but in all the time I watched them not one faltered or fell back. If a muscling cross-current caught them amidships they just surrendered to the force for a second then drove back against it with a quick double or triple pulse of the tail, returning effortlessly to their former position. Sometimes a drowned insect or caterpillar would drift within range of a quick thrusting grab. The fish shot forward, the white lips flashed and the morsel was gone. Then, instead of turning, the chub simply hung almost limply and fell back with the current to its allotted place in the shoal.

I must have watched for almost an hour, becoming half mesmerized by the rhythmic sway of the fish and the turbulence of the water. Then, all at once, the entire shoal began to sink down. They didn't suddenly dive or turn away; they simply melted into the depths and were lost from sight. A movement on the riverside path caught my eye and I turned to see two anglers walking by, passing without noticing me in the willow. They trudged steadily along, obviously finished with their day and not even attempting caution. The fish had detected the vibrations of their footfalls even before they came into sight.

I was magnetically attracted by any puddle, ditch, pond or canal. Just the look of the water itself could hold my attention long enough to drive a normal parent to distraction, but when I discovered the presence of fish even a tractor couldn't have hauled me away. Living water contained all kinds of wonderful mysteries and, when I began fishing, these mysteries were almost all I needed to keep me eagerly casting from dawn to dusk. And, though I soon had enough fish lore to be able to guess the potential of a given water, rational thinking was not allowed to cloud my imagination. I saw myself hooking a monster at each place I fished, though the real mystery was why I fished some of those places at all.

There was a sullen stream with a sandy bed flowing through a wood I knew, half an hour's bike ride from home. It was tremendously exciting because someone told me the story of a gigantic trout that lived there. This monster had eaten all the smaller fish, which was why you never saw any signs of life, even if you crept along the bank when the sun was high, hoping to see familiar shapes moving over the pale sandy bottom. You would never see the big trout either. He was too canny to be caught out in the open like that. But he was hungry, so if you fished with strong tackle, in the wood, where it was dark and where the stream ran deeper between the roots of old trees, you might be lucky and hook him.

'What bait should I use?'

'Bacon rind if you can't find a dead bird or a mouse.'

So I fished with bacon rind and never had a bite all day, nor sensed any life whatsoever in the dark, slow water. Of course it was just a myth, though even such a hollow myth can make a stream seem deeper and more magical than it really is.

I remember another stream, a crystalline chalk stream which flowed out of a wide, lily-covered millpond. It ran through a deep, densely overgrown wood, criss-crossed with mossy fallen boughs, shrouded by willows and alders, hemmed in by reeds and ferns, inhabited by tigerish pike, little dace, black-tailed chub and a solitary pioneering sea trout. It was a boy's paradise, a completely enclosed and secret world which I explored all day and never saw another soul nor quite tunnelled through to the wood's far side. What became of the stream? Was there another lake? Did it run into a river? Was it joined by other streams to become a river itself? After rippling through one willow thicket, the stream turned and ran into another, bend after bend, pool after pool, all of them demanding careful inspection. I only fell in twice.

There were small, sunlit clearings where the water sparkled and the banks were yellow with kingcups and iris. Entering one of these, I saw a pike of about five or six pounds basking near the surface of a shallow glide. Alongside it was a portly chub almost as big. They made a weird pair, like a wart-hog living with a wolf or a marriage between Queen Victoria and Count Dracula.

Eventually the stream flowed through a tunnel under the embankment of a disused railway. Through the brick archway I could see the water gliding on into a continuation of the wood but the water was too deep to wade and the tangle of nettles and brambles on the embankment too thick to penetrate. Next

21

Just as I hoped, he started to approach me.

It ran through a deep, densely overgrown wood, criss-crossed with fallen boughs.

time, if I came earlier, I would find a way across. Through the tunnel the wood looked brighter, even more enchanting.

But there were too many other lovely places to explore and after that first, thrilling discovery, I never went back. (So often, I never went back.)

On most unpolluted English rivers there is the myth of the giant pike. By the time I was twelve I was familiar with some of the best of these tales: how a pike attacked a cow at a cattle drink; how a vengeful beast had taken the finger or hand of an angler: how a swimming dog or swan had just disappeared. I read about the girl on her honeymoon, trailing her fingers in the water as her husband rowed her upstream of Fordingbridge. A huge pike grabbed her and severed the third finger of the left hand, but later an angler caught the monster and found the wedding ring still in its gullet. Of course it was returned to the rightful owner.

I did not catch any big pike myself, nor really tried, for I have never felt drawn to pike as I have to other species. But then, how can you be drawn to something like a flesh-eating dinosaur? I have certainly been impressed by pike, by their beautiful markings and colouring, sometimes striped, sometimes spotted, silver, green and gold; and there is an awful fascination about the malevolent marble-sized eyes, high set in the primaeval crocodile head. But what impresses most is their terrible hair-trigger stillness, the stillness of something that is patiently deciding not whether to kill, but when and what to kill. The quivering intensity of even a small pike is as sinister as anything in nature, more so than the quiet watchfulness of a coiled snake or the science-fiction creepiness of a praying mantis. When you glimpse a twenty-pounder shadowing the depths it can make your mouth go dry, especially when you are only a lad and the pike is as long as you. It was a pike that gave me one of the best shocks of my life.

There was a fish of about fifteen pounds, basking at the surface near a patch of lilies, twenty feet from the bank. I could see every stripe along its lean back; the tail was motionless but the pectorals swayed at about the same rate as the pendulum of a grandfather clock. His placid appearance belied his murderous heart. He was like Genghis Khan reclining in a deck-chair, but his eyes gave him away. He could not disguise the expression of a bloody tyrant, even though he

24

seemed to be fooling a shoal of little roach.

For the sake of those silly fish it was important that I play a joke on the old savage and ruffle his scales a bit. Very carefully I inched forward until I could just touch the water with the toe of my right boot. Then I began gently rippling the surface, hoping the pike, with its aggressive curiosity and fixed focus, would confuse the boot with a water vole or a duckling. The ruse had an immediate, spine-tingling effect. The pike had been lying parallel to the bank but as soon as the first ripples spread out over the calm surface he began to bristle visibly. He was like a hungry spider responding to the appetizing vibrations of its web. All the fins began to quiver and as the fish swung slowly round I could feel the pressure of those one-track eyes as they picked out the small bobbing mouthful under the bank.

Just as I hoped, he started to approach me, obviously not seeing or sensing anything but my boot. It was an almost imperceptible forward motion, leaning rather than swimming, with the head lower than the tail. As he got to about ten feet from me I prepared his surprise, intending to suddenly kick out and send the water flying. But the boot was on the other foot.

As I shifted my balance to make the kick, the pike launched itself at me. One minute it was a drifting log, the next it was a torpedo blowing me out of the water. Though I was balancing for a forward kick I converted the manoeuvre into a flailing backward somersault — the sort of thing that's impossible to describe and only possible to do when being attacked by a man-eater.

There was a violent splash, but when I'd rolled over and jumped upright again I saw only ripples, bubbles and a cloud of disturbed mud. I looked down at my feet and they were both still there.

CHAPTER THREE

Minnows

I was haunted by monsters but plagued by minnows. They were the only result of all my early river expeditions and I longed to catch something more in keeping with my dreams. Of course there had been a time, in the very beginning, when minnows were welcomed with open fingers, when each specimen was individually marvelled at in a jam jar – a sparkling creation of nature that had also become my creation. By catching the fleeting shadows in the water I made them real. However, after the first few hundred, one minnow began to look very much like another. When I cast for something grander and they refused to stop biting I became irritated, regarding them as one of nature's little aberrations, like Brussels sprouts or school prefects.

I would set forth in the morning, hoping that the chub or roach which swam in my imagination would soon become a reality. Just a single example of a proper river fish and I could call myself a proper angler. But all I found were the hordes of minnows, confirming my rank as a first-class tiddler snatcher. Whatever I used for bait, the eager, stupid little creatures got it all in the end. I once came home at the end of a day's fishing with the minnows still swimming in my head. It led to a nightmare in which an eternal river of minnows flowed into a seething ocean of them. If it had not been for my village pond where I could always catch perch and gudgeon I might have gone mad.

Perhaps I might have stopped fishing the rivers altogether were it not for the occasional visitation by some illustrious creature. I was once captivated by the sight of a large solitary roach drifting through a minnow shoal, like a yacht cleaving through canoes. And once a tremendous perch, with his spiked fin hoisted like a banner, loomed up from a deep hole and sent the minnows exploding through the surface and into the air. Also there were those intense, serious-faced men who performed the miracle of fishing for an entire day without catching a single minnow. As I recall, it was unusual for them to catch anything, but if they did it was always something staggering, like a bream too huge to cram into a keepnet.

My younger brother Nick often came fishing with me and it was he, with amazing panache, who caught the first non-minnow. We went to the Wey near Godalming, where the river winds slowly across open fields and down long avenues of alder. We discovered a shoal of chub skulking in a cove of overhanging brambles and rushed to set up our rods. Instead of fiddling about with our standard float gear, as I was doing, Nick simply tied on a hook, baited with a worm, dropped it over the bank and instantly connected with an authentic rod-bender. He didn't exclaim at all! I remember hearing his feet scrunch in the undergrowth when he struck and when I looked round the curve of his rod was unbelievable. It was a living curve, not the usual fixed bend after the line had been cast into a tree or caught round a snag on the bottom.

The fish jagged about a bit then wallowed on the surface. We had no net but Nick managed to lift it up over the brambles and onto the grass, where we fell on it with boggled eyes. A tremendous, minnow-dwarfing, brassy-flanked chub of at least a pound.

Soon after this great event we fished a wooded stretch of a small Sussex river and found yet another shoal of aristocrats. This time they were dace, all much bigger than run-of-the-mill dace, and there was a corker at the head of the shoal which was as big or bigger than Nick's chub. As far as I was concerned, a dace like that would have fulfilled the fishing dreams of an entire season.

We had some maggots, which the fish began to take enthusiastically by the handful, yet when we cast they took not the slightest interest in our hookbaits, presented confidently on a size 10 to 6-pound line, in gin-clear water. We couldn't understand it. After a thousand or so casts my float finally bobbed half under and out came the inevitable minnow.

Below a tree on the opposite bank, just ten yards away, a float was suspended in mid-air, evidence of some past miscast. The fact that we couldn't actually see the line attached to the float meant it was finer than ours, which was about as

visible as parcel string. We remarked on this because we remembered reading how dace prefer fine tackle and had to admit that our gear was not as delicate as it might have been. Therefore we couldn't refuse what providence was dangling in front of us.

Downstream was a little weir, which I waded across in bare feet. I walked up to the tree and was confronted by a large noticeboard nailed to the trunk. Private Fishing E. A. S. Bailiff T. E. Wheeler. We had seen dozens of such notices before (in fact there was one exactly the same on our own bank), but we were never bothered by them, even though we were not members of the E. A. S. or any other angling society. However, there was something about that sign which oppressed me. I was not happy about it, though I could not say why. Perhaps it was the fact that it was newly painted that gave me an uncharacteristic twinge of guilt. Then I remembered the dace. They were of a higher order than the E. A. S. or T. E. Wheeler and by fishing for them I would likewise rise above such petty considerations. So I climbed the tree, using the noticeboard to pull myself up, and, without falling in, I recovered the float, line *and* hook. As expected, the line was ludicrously fine and the hook, though rusty, squintingly small. The float was a six-inch porcupine quill and within a few minutes the whole assembly was attached by a dubious knot to my reel line. The dace were

Downstream was a little weir where I could wade
across in barefeet.

Once a tremendous perch loomed up from a deep hole.

still eager for maggots; the float sailed over their heads and then zipped under. I struck, there was a silver flash deep down and then one in my head as, for the first time ever, I saw a fish-induced bend forming in my rod. It was a whale of a dace, a Zeppelin of a dace. I had hooked the big one, though to be truthful it was probably only the second or third biggest. Because of the fragile tackle, I restrained myself from trying to heave the fish straight up onto the bank and it darted and plunged around excitingly. Then, just as it quietened, something terrible appeared on the surface, something more menacing than a monstrous pike, a crocodile or a German U-boat. We were only looking at an inverted reflection, but because of the way it had bristled into view I was certain it was none other than Bailiff T. E. Wheeler. We both looked up at him standing on the opposite bank, next to the tree with the ominous sign. The expression of official disdain coupled with the stance of a storm trooper were painful to our eyes.

'Stay there!' he barked. 'I'm coming round!'

My lovely dace flapped like a silver pennant on the surface, but there was not time to land and admire him. I jerked the hook free and he swirled and dived, taking my heart with him.

We ran off through the woods and I returned to my status as a minnow snatcher.

CHAPTER FOUR

Across the Thames

~

T he only sound to break the quiet of the dawn and the only thing to break the broad surface of the Thames was the little ferry as it chugged slowly across from the boatyard towards the south gate of Hampton Court Park. The sun was up but there was still a thin layer of mist after a cool night and the river appeared as serene as it must always have looked before the coming of the motor launch and the concreting of the banks.

Nick and I had not fished the Thames before, nor did we wish to do so then, however promising it looked. It was our intention to follow the advice of an older angler (aged fifteen) and fish the Long Water in the park. There amongst the lilies we would find tench, perch, rudd, pike and, most longed for of all, carp.

We disembarked and, as the ferry turned and burbled away into the lifting mist, we hesitated, almost allowing the river to tempt us. But whatever wonders might be hidden below the slowly moving surface there was obviously nothing to equal a Long Water carp. We passed through the gate and entered a different world altogether. Again there was a thin layer of mist, but instead of obscuring the bleaker aspects of an urbanized river it only enhanced an already delightful scene. There were ancient, solitary trees, a circular reed-fringed pool, a distant avenue, a herd of grazing deer, all on the edge of a hazy reality. No other person intruded upon this paradise. It was entirely our own.

We skirted the pool and came upon another pool – or was it merely a mist-filled hollow? Then, after a brief walk, we reached the head of the Long Water and stood for a while, our gaze drawn by the narrow perspective of avenue and lake receding into a misty vanishing-point. We chose to fish the west bank and

crept along it for a hundred yards, trying to decide which gap in the lilies to cast into. The plate-sized pads roofed all kinds of mysterious stirrings and sudden violent upheavals that skimmed the leaves sideways and spread a great half-circle of ripple across the open centre channel. What creatures were hidden there?

We peered into openings beween pads and scanned the narrow, irregular channel along the margins. A large rudd with an olive-green back and blood-red fins drifted tantalizingly into view. We were startled by a pike that barged into a circular clearing almost under our noses. Its eyes swivelled as it spotted us and it vanished as suddenly as it had appeared, leaving a miniature whirlpool. But the hoped-for materialization of carp and tench did not occur, though we spent half the morning watching and waiting.

Eventually we tackled up and for a while were entertained simply by the sight of our two crow quills, one red the other yellow, poised dramatically on the edge of the lilies. Great fish stirred nearby and it was surely just a matter of time before something overwhelming happened. Of course we'd be smashed to bits in the submarine jungle, but this didn't matter. We knew we could live quite happily with the memory of such a superb disaster. However, when you are young and excited an hour is an unbearably long time for nothing to happen. Even your greatest hopes can evaporate if your float refuses to move during those eternal,

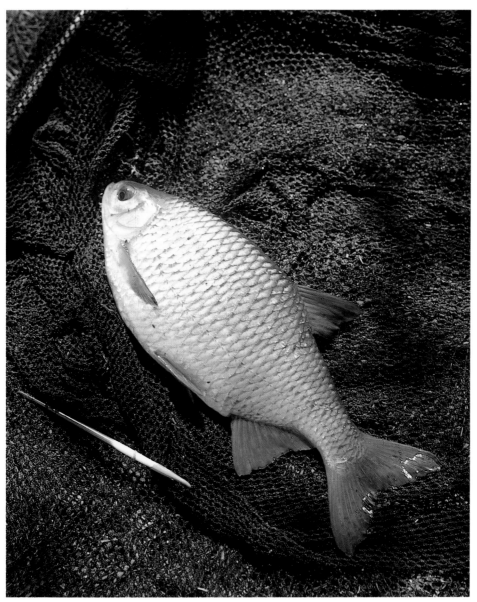

A large rudd with olive green back and blood red fins drifted tantalisingly into view.

watchful minutes. The sun went in, the fish stopped quaking the lilies and the lake began to look less mysterious. By sandwich time the excitement and drama were over and we began thinking that perhaps the river was the place to fish after all. We knew that the lower Thames was not noted for its minnow fishing; therefore, if we caught anything at all, it would obviously be wonderful.

We marched back to the riverside gate, but while the parkland now looked nearly ordinary in the grey afternoon light the Thames looked positively dismal. There was no colour, no life, just the slow sliding of dark water, unruffled, unhurried and seemingly uninhabited.

I think our shoulders drooped a bit. It was probably not even worth the attempt and we wondered whether we should give our parents the shock of their lives and come home early from a day's fishing. We remembered that our more experienced friend had fished with some success on the Thames, catching roach and dace on leger tackle. We had not fished the leger before, but decided we might as well give it a try while we waited for the ferry. Though we would probably not catch anything we could at least say we had mastered a new technique.

The only legers we possessed were a couple of half-ounce coffin leads and we cast these far out, as if we were beach fishing for cod. They hit the surface with an impressive smack and we put the rods down, wondering what was meant to happen next. If a fish obliged, would the line merely quiver or would the rod get dragged into the water? It didn't matter either way as there seemed as much chance of catching a fish as finding a conker in the Sahara.

An old man on a bicycle came riding up the bankside path, a great creel over one shoulder, a bulky rod holdall over the other.

'Afternoon, lads,' he said cheerily and waved. But at the precise moment of only single-handed control his front wheel hit a stone or a twig and he teetered, swerved and so nearly went into the river.

'Blimey!' he said, as he straightened himself out. He pedalled off again a bit shakily and I turned to Nick to say what a shame it was. Nick agreed; another inch, he said, and the old buffer would have made a beautiful splash. We laughed but were instantly silenced by a movement in Nick's rod. We stared, waiting for the phenomenon to repeat itself. It didn't, but when Nick began to reel in he suddenly shouted, 'I've got one!'

Something came across the surface as limply as a drowned leaf. It even looked like one when Nick lifted it out – a drowned, brown leaf.

'What is it? A dead perch?'

I shuffled through the memorized edition of my *Brooke Bond Album of Freshwater Fish* and declared:

'It's a ruffe!'

This was an important event after all, a serious capture to be written up in the diary with red ink and capital letters. The Thames was not as dull as it appeared.

A short time later my own rod jagged and though I was slow to respond I still connected with something. It must have looked as if I was reeling in a significant fish, yet there was only the vaguest sensation of life in the bent rod. There was certainly more weight than I had cast out, but little resistance. A curious shape broke surface, even curiouser than a ruffe, and when Nick saw what it was he cackled with laughter. A large freshwater mussel had clamped itself over the coffin lead, and yet as I prepared to lift it out we saw, to our amazement, something else on the line. Up onto the bank came the mussel, and, gleaming silver, the first and most wondrous dace in the history of the world.

CHAPTER FIVE

A Flurry of Rivers

Lucky is the boy whose fishing is within walking distance of his home. Fortunate is he who has a river or lake within easy biking distance. Countless are they who suffer the frustration of being unable to reach their fishing without motorized transport. Public transport demands time, money and organization; no self respecting fisher-boy can afford to even consider these things. Parental transport, presuming there is such a thing, not only demands effective pleading, it also depends on the time available to the parent. It's wonderful that they are kind and generous enough to take you fishing, but there are usually conditions attached, like the obvious setting of time limits. You'll rarely be at the water early enough to see the dawn mists and you cannot make the tenth last cast into the sunset if your parent is just preparing to drive off without you.

I was lucky. Not only did I have an excellent little pond less than a mile from home, I also had the River Mole within easy bicycling reach. The Thames at Kingston was only a sixpenny bus ride away and my parents were both teachers with long summer holidays and a liking for walking at faraway places. While they went off to explore an old village or a new landscape, Nick and I would fish for the day, having been dropped off at any likely-looking river on the way and collected again in the evening. In this way we fished many new, unfamiliar waters, although it was unusual ever to visit these places more than once, however much we wished to. We understood this and could even appreciate the special poignancy of fishing a delectable water with the knowledge that there would be no return. It made the day seem priceless.

Though we were grateful for these opportunities, it would have been impossible to have arranged all our fishing round these occasional excursions in the old family car. It wasn't simply that the locations depended on parental whim; the car really was old and it didn't respond kindly to excessive demands. (It broke down once on a long journey westwards and we got terribly upset as there wasn't any fishing for miles.) So we went regularly to our local pond, there to participate in the high art of gudgeon fishing and the even higher art of perch fishing. And we also went to feed our dreams, for we always knew we were in the presence of mythical, colossal, uncatchable carp. And when the summer holidays arrived we would bundle up our tackle, pile into the Morris Eight and chug off into the dawn.

Our parents were, and still are, especially fond of the rugged landscapes of Wales, the Lake District, Dartmoor and Exmoor, areas veined with fast-running rivers and streams, but where the fishing was mostly for the lesser species – salmon and trout. We didn't mind fishing for silver tourists and spotty herberts, as we called them; in fact, a big silver tourist was always entertaining when hooked on a roach rod and 6-pound line, and it was great fun to stalk trout in a gushing mountain stream. But we preferred rivers with more varied pleasures, where we might find the species dearer to our hearts. Also, we had proved that it was a mark of higher achievement to hook a big roach or chub than a trout or a salmon. We had rarely succeeded with the former, yet with the latter, in the right conditions, it was almost impossible to fail.

We understood why the fly fisherman handicaps himself when he could more efficiently catch trout or salmon with a worm: the fish were as daft as minnows, the salmon especially. I had offered floating crusts to a certain big carp countless times during a single summer, without any response, yet the first time I offered a piece of bread to a big wild trout he almost jumped out of the water to grab it. Rather than handicap themselves with flies, why, we wondered, could these obviously skilful anglers not fish for something more worthwhile? Was it simply that they were fond of eating their catch? This seemed a reasonable notion for there was no harm in taking salmonids. However, it was tantamount to murder if you killed a carp. Of course, had we grown up by the Tay or the Test we might have had a different attitude.

I confess, too, that we had been mildly prejudiced by our growing angling

library. Though we had read some great books by trout and salmon anglers we were obviously more interested in reading about the kind of fishing we enjoyed most. Our mentor was Richard Walker. He had wonderful things to say about carp, roach, chub and the rest. We were later to discover that he was enthusiastic about trout, but he did not, in the fifties and sixties, write much about them. When he wrote about salmon he was disparaging and sometimes scathing, which didn't help to alleviate the vague sense of regret whenever we set forth on some well stocked salmon water. Though we were sure to enjoy ourselves and catch a few fish, we would rather have gone to the Wey, the Arun or the Stour to get tipsy on dace and roach.

Later on we modified our views on fly fishing, or at least I did, Nick being an incurable fundamentalist. I learnt how to fish the dry fly and was immediately won over by its charm. It was, after all, quite an advantage to be able to cast a tiny imitation insect across the river without making even the smallest splash. The chub and dace were deceived almost as completely as the trout. But I never really accepted salmon fishing as a worthwhile occupation. Though I admitted that the salmon was a marvellous, powerful creature with a fascinating life cycle, I couldn't fish wholeheartedly for it knowing that it never actually fed once in from the sea. It seemed almost unfair to take advantage of its aggressive bad temper and taunt it with gaudy spinners or flies just so that it would snap at them. Rather than provoke a fish to bite I preferred the more subtle art of deception.

Despite our preference for cyprinids, we did savour some marvellous trout and salmon fishing in rivers like the Duddon, in Cumberland, the Teifi, in Wales, and the Exe in Devon, as well as numerous little streams and rivers whose names we never knew or have since forgotten. And, though we came to accept this alternative style of fishing, there were occasions when our holidays took us to genuine dream rivers, like the time we were dumped on the banks of the Severn, near Shrewsbury. It looked a scintillating stretch of water, fast, crystal-clear, luxuriantly weeded, with deep glides, sparkling shallows, overgrown islands and high, willow-hung banks.

Upstream of the road bridge where our parents had dropped us was a man who said he was barbel fishing and we paused a moment in our headlong rush to find a casting place. We had seen all kinds of fishermen fishing for all kinds of fish, but this was something we had never witnessed before. The angler cast worm-baited leger tackle well up and across and let the current take it down and round so that it bumped across the gravel in a long arc and settled for a minute under his own bank. It was a much more active and vigorous style of fishing than we were used to seeing on the slow-flowing rivers back home. He was an obviously skilful angler who cast with such confident expectancy that we could hardly tear ourselves away. There would have been hallelujahs had we seen our first barbel, but we had our own fishing to attend to and perhaps we might just catch a barbel ourselves ...

Where the river swept round a bend there was a small willow-grown island. I looked at the slack water at the island's tail and decided it looked distinctly exciting. Out went a freelined worm, which, on the third or fourth cast, was grabbed as it hit the water. A great fish shot downstream, got into the main current and made me think it was a silver tourist. We had bought a landing net that season and now Nick came running up with it, arriving next to me just as a

'Chub'! We shouted, overjoyed that it wasn't a salmon.

We savoured some marvellous trout and salmon fishing.

brassy flank showed on the surface, far out.

'Chub!' we shouted, overjoyed that it wasn't a salmon. (Off course it could have been a barbel, which would have made us even more joyful.) We eventually landed it, with a flurry of spray and a few whoops of jubilation. Another angler came up, congratulated me, produced a pocket spring balance and officially weighed the specimen. Nick and I stood back and kept our voices down. This was a serious yet not a truly earth-shattering matter and we pretended to be solemn and indifferent, as though we were accustomed to catching such dazzling fish. The final pronouncement was three pounds and two ounces and after the travelling scalesman had walked off I did a few somersaults along the bank.

We didn't have another bite all day, not that we cared. Our mother, mindful of the value of the angler's every moment, came to collect us as late as possible, bless her.

'Did you have an enjoyable day?' she asked.

'Fantastic,' I said. 'When I'm old enough I'm going to buy a motor bike, leave home and spend all summer here.'

How old do you have to be? I made that vow thirty years ago and still haven't been back.

In 1959, on the River Frome, we were shown the best method for catching trout. We were on holiday in Dorset and while our parents spent the morning shopping at Dorchester we had a walk along the river, with our tackle at the ready. We came in sight of a boy of about our age who was dancing about on the bank. As we approached we could see he was stuffing something into his trouser pocket. It was a fish, in fact quite a large fish – a trout of about two pounds – but his pocket was too small and the fish was stuck. It explained all the jiggling about. But the trout would not be joggled completely in.

'Are you club members!' he asked, nervously, glancing at our rods.

We admitted that we were not and he immediately relaxed and grinned. The tail of the trout remained dangling.

'The bailiff took my rod and reel,' he said. 'Then he took my trout and said if he catches me here again he'll take my life!'

There was a quiet interval while we considered these words.

'Will he take our rods?' we asked.

'Not if you don't use 'em,' he said. 'Hide 'em in the bushes and just bring a spool of line and some big hooks. I'll show 'en what to do.'

Nick and I hesitated, exchanging meaningful glances. Then we nodded and smiled and the little poacher laughed. He led the way along the well tended banks and then up onto a bridge, where we craned over the stone parapet and looked down at a wondrous sight. In the deep clear pool below were at least half a dozen big brown trout. We had seen some large herberts in our time, but some of these looked two feet long.

'Now watch this,' said the poacher.

He took out a ball of squeezed breadflake from his (other) pocket, pinched out a knob of crumb and dropped it straight down. Before it had sunk more than a few inches two trout rose simultaneously. There was a violent swirl and the bread was gone. The boy said he had stood on the bridge one evening and watched a man with a rod 'That must've cost ten pound' cast a fly over the trout till after sunset. 'It was shocking! They didn't even look at it.'

Following his instructions, I tied a big hook to my line, squeezed a lump of flake over it and lowered it into the water. A big trout sidled casually over and up, the great mouth gaped and the next second I felt as if I'd been rapped on the knuckles with an axe. The line was wrapped round my hand and as the trout turned and bolted I was almost cut to the bone. I yelled, all the fish remembered urgent business elsewhere and the one I was attached to shot up under the bridge. The line hit the stonework and broke instantly. I was appalled at losing the trout, but relieved that my hand was still in one piece. The poacher was almost indignant.

'What kind of line do you call that?' he snorted.

'Luron Two,' I said, 'six pounds breaking strain.'

'Six pounds!' he chortled. 'Here, this's what I use.'

Coiled round a bit of stick was about twenty yards of the coarsest, thickest nylon line we had ever seen.

'My dad uses it for conger,' he said.

As we waited for the trout to recover from the drama a brown van came over the bridge, slowed down, then continued on its way. A short while later a man strolled up to us and by the way our new found friend reacted we knew he was the bailiff.

'Not fishing, are you?' he asked and his eyebrows rose to the top of his forehead.

He didn't look truly evil, yet this was a man who could confiscate your tackle and your life. We held out our hands, a look of sublime innocence on our faces. Not having a rod and reel did wonders for our confidence, despite the fact that I could still see the tell-tale scars across my palm. But there was a more damning piece of evidence and as we remembered it and he suddenly noticed it the sun went in, the river darkened, a distant bell began solemnly tolling and three vultures descended from the clouds.

It was the pocketful of trout.

CHAPTER SIX

The Float

T he day was over and I stood on the little bridge with a group of other anglers, waiting for the bus home. All around us the wide expanses of the Pevensey Levels were seeping up the gold of the evening sun. The River Haven wound imperceptibly towards us, the current barely strong enough to stir the reeds or move the lilies.

I was the only fisher-boy present; the others were mostly middle-aged men, their creels, holdalls and bags piled up on one side of the bridge while they leant over the other, facing the sun. Some were smoking pipes and the strong smell of the tobacco hung in the calm air, mingling with the fainter scent of the river. We were watching that rare specimen, the fisher-girl. She was sitting on the bank below us, quite unperturbed by our presence, a confident nine- or ten-year-old who handled her tackle with a studied nonchalance, flicking an orange and green float out to the edge of a small lily bed. It settled perfectly, with just the right amount of shot to hold it stationary in the slow current. With mild interest, the men watched the float while quietly discussing the high and low points of their day. They mused on the river's imperfections as well as its charms, praising its bream but cursing its eels, pleased about its roach, mystified by its tench.

The float bobbed, cutting short the conversation. All the while the anglers had been talking it had been the dominant feature in the landscape; now, after a wonderfully dramatic pause, it began to dominate the conversation.

'I reckon it'll go right under in a second,' whispered one.

'It's probably only an eel,' said another.

'She'll put us all to shame. I saw bream bubbles down there a minute ago.'

The girl smiled to herself, as if she knew she was about to astonish us.

The bus was late, not that anyone minded. The evening began to cool, causing the river to invisibly steam and strengthen that fragrance we had been half
aware of all day. It was like a mixture of bruised mint, strawberries and wet
mud. The girl sat on the grass, still faintly smiling. In the twenty minutes we
had been watching the float had bobbed twice and slid perhaps two inches across
the surface, almost enough for her to react to. It seemed she had prepared to
strike, but then, as the movement ceased, she relaxed again and everyone fell
back into their watchful trance. One or two of the men looked merely amused
at the spectacle of a little girl trying to catch a fish, but most were as hypnotized
as I.

In the last minutes before the bus finally appeared no one spoke at all. The evening was utterly silent. The river became almost painfully bright and seemed to be flowing from the base of the sun. The men's faces turned gold. The little orange float was just a black splinter in the reflections and I thought it comic but also wonderful the way it was mesmerizing us, who had just spent a whole day watching our own floats. But there is something very compelling about someone else's float, especially in such circumstances, when there was not just the one impartial observer, but a whole audience, all reacting as if we were watching a bit of theatre, completely absorbed by the plot, eager to know how it would unfold.

Perhaps the bus would never come, nor the float ever go under, as it seemed to me that the world had already gone on without us and time had stopped on the Haven. Suddenly I was convinced that the girl was going to catch a fish and stared at the float even more intently.

A distant rumble broke the spell and we turned to see the bus come slowly into view. It stopped by the bridge and after collecting our gear we all piled aboard. As the bus pulled away the girl waved, acknowledging us for the first and last time. We left her in the sunmelt, disappointed at not knowing the end of the story....

The evening was utterly still.

CHAPTER SEVEN

Total Eclipse

A Cautionary Tale

I magine a river so perfectly clear it was invisible and only by putting your hand in it could you tell it was there, only by watching the fish drifting through it could you define its course. The River Waveney in Suffolk used to be almost like that and if you gazed at the water from certain angles where there was no glare, ripple or reflection it was not easy to say where the air finished and the water began.

I first visited this river when I was sixteen. At that time, in the mid-sixties, it was one of the most famous roach rivers in the country and for someone who had never caught a roach over a pound it was a revelation. The water being so transparent, the fish were ridiculously easy to find, even though there were numerous dense beds of weed and lilies. Everywhere I looked, or so it seems in retrospect, there were roach, gliding through the depths on their crimson-coloured fins. Worming through the bankside herbage and getting my face an inch above the surface I was able to gaze straight down into one clear pool, where a dozen or so large fish circled languidly in the slow current. The sun was shining on the sandy riverbed and the fish, lit from below as well as above, looked ethereal.

For as long as our stay lasted I was going to be an impassioned roach angler. Nick and I had cycled out from the ancient farmhouse where the family was staying for that year's holiday and for the first few hours of our exploration we wandered around getting slightly drunk on all the incredible visions. We had read about places like this but had always been mildly sceptical. Of course we believed in big roach; they were something that came to a very lucky angler if he fished diligently for the whole of his life. We had seen a roach that had been officially weighed in at 1 pound 12 ounces, so we knew what we were believing in. But we were not absolutely convinced by the legendary sort of waters that an angling writer like Richard Walker would describe, where during an evening's fishing one could always expect a brace of two-pounders. However, the Waveney immediately established the truth of the legends and we thought it feasible to catch a dozen two-pounders before tea.

The river meandered through wide, rolling cornfields and flowed round from the south-west towards a high pine-crowned hill, where it split into two. The northern arm, really a backwater, ran for nearly a quarter of a mile before curving back into the main river, thus forming an island. This was the place we chose to fish, having first thoroughly explored it, creeping all round its grassy and reedy edges and gazing upon the red-fins that surrounded us. Where the main river flowed past an orchard I discovered a shoal of fish which averaged about a pound, with perhaps one or two going twice that size. I thought it best to cast for them first rather than try for one of the groups of grandfathers. The sun was high and though my roach-fishing experience was limited I knew that the bigger fish were not likely to begin feeding until evening. Initially it would be wiser to concentrate on the smaller specimens, watching their reactions to my imperfect technique; later I would fish more confidently for the giants.

Nick had stumbled on a shoal of enormous dace and could not resist having a go at them, despite the fact that he had been tossing maggots at a pound roach and watching it chase them downstream. I was about to cast when I heard him shout out that he had just caught the biggest dace in the world.

The roach by the orchard were cunning. When a dozen maggots came wafting downstream they would appear boldly from the weeds, then rapidly shy away again while my little quill danced down behind, carrying two grubs on a size 12. Once or twice a little roachlet would approach the bait, harrying it with sharp jabs, but even he would not take it properly. So I scaled down to a line of 1 pound breaking strain and attached a smaller hook. Instant success! The roachlet was soon sparkling in the grass. My first fish from the Waveney, about four inches long. There followed a series of missed opportunities, with the larger

roach definitely making a play for the hookbait. Then, at the end of the swim, I saw a dark shape slide across the current, zip the float under and then break surface as I hooked it. It flashed silver as I held it gently back from the weeds and coaxed it gradually up, nearer and nearer to the waiting net. Then it was in the mesh and on the bank and I could praise the natural miracle of a genuine one-pound roach.

Neither of us caught anything larger that day but the next we both landed several superb fish to almost a pound and a half and I watched a huge roach make a lightning grab for my bait, only to miss it on the strike. We had five more days to fish and were confident that those elusive shadows in the deeper pools would soon become the tangible two-pounders in our landing nets. However, because of an unexpected earthquake the entire Waveney and all its roach disappeared from the face of the earth.

I have said that we were staying at a farmhouse. We were looked after by a

Nick had stumbled on a shoal of enormous dace.

Then it was in the mesh and on the bank and I could
praise a natural miracle.

friendly farmer's wife who was helped in her work by two lovely daughters. Need I really say more?

Because of my passion for fishing I had managed to avoid the tricky subject of the opposite sex throughout the early years of my adolescence. So, when I returned from our first day on the Waveney, and was served supper by a beautiful fifteen-year-old girl with blue eyes and a warm smile, I was so preoccupied by thoughts of roach that I scarcely noticed her. But on the next evening the same eyes confronted me in the twilight as I was putting my bike in the barn. Foolishly, I spoke to them and they sparkled. The effect on me was surprising: it was as if I had seen a three-pound roach, except that I suddenly realized that I was the roach. She was fishing for me and now I had seen deep into those mesmerizing eyes and been rendered speechless by that beautiful smile I was firmly hooked. The worst of it was I did not even put up a fight. I came in like a tame bream.

It was worse than an earthquake. My angling world suffered a seemingly total eclipse. I had seen this kind of phenomenon before but never expected it would happen to me. Earlier that summer, on a classic tench morning, I hurried round to a friend's home at the prearranged hour and, as was our custom, threw pebbles at his window to get him up. Eventually the window opened, his sleepy head emerged into the sunrise and he uttered the immortal words:

'Wendy and I are going to Bognor.'

Who was Wendy? Were there tench at Bognor? What had happened to this fanatical angler in the last three days since I'd seen him? I cycled off to the tench pond alone and perplexed. He had obviously gone mad, having offered to sell me all his rods and, without even blinking, admitted that he had fallen in love. It was as if he had undergone a metamorphosis and became a different person altogether.

And I too became a different person. Overnight I had lost my identity. I was not an angler any more and did not even want to think about fishing. Though I did not know who I was, never having experienced this state of heart before, I knew that it was essential to be permanently in the presence of that magical girl.

Nick soon got over the shock of seeing his elder brother's decline. In fact he struck up a happy relationship with the younger sister and then also lost his sense of priorities. We did not go back to the Waveney again that year.

It was 150 miles from the farm to our home, which meant that there would be long, painful interludes between meetings. After the bitterness at parting at the end of the summer holidays, the joy of our reunion back at the farmhouse for Christmas was enough to make even a sentimentalist ill. There followed a bleak spring full of earnest and impassioned letters, then the promise of summer.

I sold a favourite rod and some tackle and bought an engine on two wheels which would probably get me as far as Suffolk and hopefully no farther. But there was still a spark of the original fire in me for I kept my old Avon rod and even took it with me on that journey, thinking there might be the odd occasion when my love and I could go fishing, perhaps in the evenings after harvest time. Nick came on the pillion as navigator and we could have got there quicker if we had gone on bicycles.

There at last was the heartening sight of the old farmhouse on the hill surrounded by woods and cornfields. However, not since the final act of *Romeo and Juliet* had a romance ended in such perfect tragedy. We rode up the long track following a post van and when we reached the farmhouse the two sisters came out to meet us. But, before I had time to even say Hello, the postman handed a letter to my sweetheart. She glanced at the handwriting on the envelope and jumped into the air, a look of terrible bliss in her eyes which she did not even try to conceal. One minute I was floating in the stratosphere, the next I was falling into a bottomless abyss. As the light went out of my life and raced off to read her letter in private, her younger sister revealed that a person called Robert had barged onto the scene during my long absence. Not only had he been obviously poisoning my name, he also had a Ford Prefect.

The best place to get over a bout of suicide was unquestionably the Waveney. As I sat in a clump of willow-herb, gazing sullenly down into the gin-clear water, I mused among other things on the differences between roach and teenage girls. Roach might be elusive, remote and even fickle but if the angler kept his wits about him and abided by the cardinal rules then once the roach had decided to bite he could be reasonably confident of success. Occasionally a fish would be lost as it came towards the net, especially if it was one of the aristocrats, but it was accepted that once a roach was in the angler's mesh it would not suddenly vanish as he stooped to lift it tenderly from the water.

Two roach drifted lazily past and I followed them with my eyes as they dropped into a deep pool upstream. Then, half an hour later, a much larger fish came by, solitary, purposeful, as though he was on an urgent mission. He too descended into the pool and he drew me out of myself just long enough. I went upstream thinking to have only a brief glance into the deep water and beheld a heart-restoring sight. There was a tremendous shoal of big roach – very big roach – and they seemed to be feeding, turning quietly one way then another as they grazed over the gravel bed six feet below the surface. The dying spark within suddenly leapt up as a bright familiar flame. It was going to be all right. I would survive. I would be able to withstand the blows of fate and the cruellest denial, for I had a Mark IV Avon, an Intrepid reel and fifty yards of 1-pound line.

Before the sun went down I was fully recovered, having caught a stunning bag of roach, including three glorious two-pounders. However, since then I have never come near to repeating this success. I may have been restored, but after that summer I could not feel quite the same about roach again.

CHAPTER EIGHT

Talking to the Water

T he River Mole runs through some very attractive country, particularly along its middle reaches, where it flows alongside and then cuts through the wooded slopes of the North Downs. Over the years I explored much of its length and got to know it so well that I eventually got on speaking terms with it.

Ten or twelve miles from home the river ran through a picturesque but not too precious estate near Cobham. The land was undulating and well wooded and in the 1960s, before the Department of (road) Transport took over the world, it was a peaceful, undisturbed place. The river twisted and turned between stands of ash, oak and elm and through thickets of alder, willow and blackthorn. Mostly it flowed deep and slow, but there were stretches of shallower water which added a bit of sparkle to the proceedings. The predominant species were dace, chub, perch, roach, minnows and pike, plus a few very large predatory trout.

Before I began fishing this bit of the Mole I realized that the best way to catch fish was by understanding their habits, but I didn't appreciate that it was equally important to understand their habitat. As I became more and more absorbed in the river, certain facts, some obvious, some obscure, became clear to me so that eventually I could say with confidence where a given species of fish would be along the stretch and whether it would be feeding or not. I was sometimes wrong, but I was correct often enough to catch fish with a consistency not known since I gave up (deliberate) minnow snatching.

As I said, I got to know the river so well I used to talk to it, engaging it in conversation on appropriate topics, subjects which were relevant to the various places we met. For instance, I could go down to a deep bend in the shade of a

great ash tree and have a rewarding discussion about perch. During the long summer afternoons I would wade the streaming shallows and we would gossip endlessly about dace. In the evening I would creep up to the glides between sunken lily beds where I knew the talk would always revolve round chub. In a slowly curling eddy I would ask questions with elderberries or breadflake and the river would reply with roach. Sometimes the river would give me a shock, suddenly shouting 'Pike' as I reeled in a dace or a perch. Then I would shout back and we would have a blazing row, which usually left me with a broken line and the river in tears for one of its little fish.

Of course it could be sulky and non-communicative. During the winter it might not talk for days, especially if it was low and the wind was in the north-east. But then a mild day of rain would change the mood completely and the river would return to its former generous, talkative self. And though most of the talk was leisurely and light-hearted we did sometimes have more profound discussions which would conclude with a four-pound chub or a two-pound perch, if I was lucky. Occasionally the river would make an obvious point about my technique and persuade me to change it. Once or twice it whispered mysteriously, urging me to cast to a spot I would never have normally chosen.

Ours was a happy relationship that would have lasted longer were it not for an even more fascinating rival – a carp pond which eventually revealed one of its best-kept secrets to me.

I remember an early autumn day, after a depressing week at school, when the river seemed to look lovelier than I'd ever seen it. It reflected the russets and yellows of the trees and also ferried these colours downstream in the first scatterings of leaves. I looked over the bridge at the familiar shoal of dace below and said good morning to them and good morning to the river. I walked upstream, encouraged by the look of optimism in my old friend, and came to a favourite pool where, earlier in the summer, I had seen a colossal chub of perhaps eight pounds. Though most of the fish I had since caught from there averaged three pounds, I was always hopeful that, one day, I might see the monster again.

The Ash Tree Pool was a pool of character, of varying depth, where the current increased in pace as it approached the stony shallows at the pool's tail. On the west side the water was deeper and there were thick beds of cabbages (sunken lilies). Along the eastern bank there was a clear run three feet deep over a bed of hard clay. The main fish-holding area was a deep hole in the cabbages where the current slowed a little before accelerating again at the head of the shallows. My plan, a fairly obvious one, was to fish from the head of the pool and run a float all along the edge of the cabbages, checking its pace at the deep hole, where the chub always waited.

In the past I had taken all my chub on freelined tackle, fished upstream and across with worms or black slugs, but with the float I could remain well hidden and yet cover more water. The first cast into a familiar productive pool is like the first question to a friend who has been on a marvellous adventure and has lots of exciting stories to tell. The red tipped porcupine quill sailed gracefully downstream while I peered out of the nettles behind it. I guessed the river would be keen to describe to me the glories of a grandfather chub, but for over an hour it ignored me, unimpressed by my new strategy. Then it began to show contempt,

*I would ask questions with bread and worms and the
river would reply with roach and chub.*

The float sailed gracefully downstream while I peered
out of the nettles behind it.

catching the tackle in lily roots and sunken branches, stealing first my hooks and then my float, an old favourite.

'All right,' I said, 'I see your point. It's not the right day for float fishing.' And I reverted to the usual freelining method, casting from the lower end of the pool and letting a lobworm trickle down into the near side of the deep hole. First throw, the line dragged in the current and slithered excitingly across the surface. I struck and the rod heaved over. Something powerful lunged into the deeps and held its position obstinately, though I could feel it wasn't snagged. Gradually the cane began to uncoil and a big chub – but not *the* big chub – came wallowing and plunging to the surface. I worked him round in a wide arc and got him in the net first try. It was a splendid, silvery four-pounder, no monster according to the universal scale of chub, but quite big enough to put my hat into the air. Especially in an enclosed, overgrown pool, it was rare to catch more than one chub during the same part of the day. It was hardly good manners to ask the river to repeat itself, let alone enlarge on the subject, particularly once it had replied positively to a question about chub. I made a couple more half-hearted casts, then wandered upstream looking for a new swim.

There were a dozen chub hanging beneath the surface in a deep eddy and I cast across to them and hooked a half-pounder. I missed a good take a few hundred yards farther up, where the river dived between high banks of dense blackthorn. I studied the long slow glide below and thought it too dark and deep to make a good chub-holding swim, especially as there was a large and shady oak reaching from bank to bank. It was as black as a tunnel. I would have gone on but, as I looked at the river, it seemed to wink at me and I knew I *must* cast there. It was astonishing how the change occurred. One moment I had dismissed the swim as worthless, the next it seemed to blaze with potential.

The worm landed under the far bank and sank down slowly towards the roots of the oak. Nothing happened to it. I cast once more and again it was not taken. Yet I wasn't disconcerted. Everything was flowing perfectly and confidently and I was in that rare state of piscatorial bliss that can counter any adversity, inspire wonders of perseverance, produce miracles of casting and eventually magic the fish onto the end of the line.

The first one weighed only a pound, but the river was wide and deep and I knew there'd be more. The second chub weighed almost five. It dived under the roots, lunged downstream, lay on the bottom and then streaked away up river, but the supple cane mastered it in the end. At the time it was not only my best chub, but the biggest fish I had ever caught.

Two more followed in quick succession, a three and a two-pounder, before my casting became mechanical and my zest for the fishing dulled.

I had never caught more than a brace of chub at a sitting before, yet I still felt that six was a bit extravagant, almost enough to give me piscatorial indigestion. (Subsequent experience only reinforced my view that fish seem to diminish in size and individual appeal when caught by the netful.) I reeled in and didn't cast again, even though I was confident I could have gone on catching fish till midnight. Indeed, because of the river's mood and the mood I was in, I felt capable of catching anything I chose anywhere along the river.

I released my netful of chub and walked back downstream, following the floating leaves and feeling I could recognize the potential of all the runs, eddies, glides and pools. Though the water was dark and mostly deep, I imagined with an intensity not known before where all the different kinds of fish would be swimming. I could almost see them. Had someone been with me I would have had to cast, to prove my point. As it was, I felt no desire to confirm what I instinctively knew. Here were roach, here were more chub, here were perch, here was a trout and a pike – and all in places I had not fished before.

Because of various known and unknown factors, including, of course, the fact that my sandwiches had been particularly fine, I had managed to overcome the usual practical problems while at the same time understanding all the messages, however coded, that the river was sending me. I felt that none of its secrets could be hidden from me and that no one, not even someone who had fished it for a lifetime, could have known it as intimately as I did then, just for those few hours. There had been flashes of insight before, but this was my first experience of the more complete awareness that is possible when the angler and his surroundings are in perfect harmony.

Yet the next time I went back to the river, we hardly spoke at all.

CHAPTER NINE

Night Fishing

~

A pale moon rose up over the treeline and as it bal-looned into the sky its reflection appeared in the lake below. Against the glow everything looked more intensely black while the lake itself came alive with tiny, moving points of light. Every bubble, no matter how small, had a miniature moon reflected on its skin and when a carp, deep down below, truffled in the mud it looked like a silent firework bursting on the surface.

My bait was down there and, at some time during the night, a carp would un-doubtedly approach it – and take it? The moment of contact could be just one moment away and that was why the night was so charged with expectancy. Everything seemed poised on the edge of – of what? A confrontation with a monster or a missed strike? A long battle and a broken line or a bland bream? The silence and the solitude only increased the tense undercurrent. There would be no sleep or relaxation, at least not for a while. And as well as the imminence of the carp there were all the other things that the mind was becoming alert to, for night is a time when every angler can come to his senses.

It was a perfect midsummer night, just like the previous night and the night before that. The air was still, heavy with scents that were hardly noticeable dur-ing the day. The water had once again seemed to become mysteriously deeper.

The occasional sounds in the undergrowth sometimes caught me unawares and I would have to think quickly to identify them: fox patter, badger rustle, hedgehog snort, deer bark, owl hoot. The weird trill of a nightjar sounded like nothing on earth. Sometimes, especially when there was no moon and no point of focus, a third eye would open and I would become supernaturally aware of an animal before it made its presence felt. And I could, on rare occasions, when this

*The silence and solitude only increased the tense
undercurrent.*

sixth sense was strongest, stalk carp even on the blackest night. I wasn't consistent, though, not like a professional dowser, homing in on water with his hazel
stick, but the same principle was involved. Anglers have marvellous opportunities to test their intuitive, instinctive powers, especially at night, in darkness
and silence, when the primary senses have nothing to latch on to.

The moon arced across the southern horizon. The line running down into the
black water never even quivered. Everything passed with an unemphatic magic
out of the night and into the cool dawn.

During the middle and late sixties I didn't feel I was getting the best out of
my fishing unless I went at night. But it had taken a while for me to become
truly at ease in the dark on my own, at my favourite carp pools, which were all
set in deep secluded woodland. During my early teens the strange beauty of the
nocturnal landscape was of less concern to me than plain self-survival.

On my first night-time foray I became seriously disturbed by the memory of
seeing a man pursued through a wood by the Devil. The man escaped, but only
because, in the film, he recalled an ancient Latin phrase which the Devil always
found distasteful. What would happen if the Devil appeared in my wood looking for likely souls? I had probably been bad enough to qualify for membership
of his club. Would I remember the magic words? Nick had remembered them
after we'd seen the film, but then he was doing Latin at school. I was doing
French, which the Devil probably didn't understand. I didn't understand it
either. Also, Nick couldn't help because he wasn't with me. It appeared that I
was doomed. If I'd had two rod rests I could have made the sign of the cross, but
I did not even have one to poke him with. Thus does the childish mind run wild
when left alone at night by a carp pool.

On another occasion, when I had grown more accustomed to the dark, I was
sitting by a secluded tree-girt pool, happily counting meteorites in the clear
sky. I had just reached twenty-one – after only an hour – when something like a
bear or a hippo crashed through the bushes behind me. The sound was so abrupt
and awful I almost fell in. The creature loomed huge in the dark, only a few
yards from where I was fishing. I thought it must be an escapee from a zoo or a
circus, but then maybe it was something *not of this earth*. It snorted heavily,
sensed me and turned its massive head towards me. The air filled with the warm

scent of its breath. However, instead of charging and trampling me, it waded placidly out through the marginal reeds. Silhouetted in the starlit water, it was revealed as nothing more menacing than a cow.

Fear of the dark is easy to understand, especially when you are young. Every ancestral voice in your head warns that the night is man's oldest enemy, but in time the fear is reasoned out. After a few frights, I managed to come to terms with fantasies and hauntings and learnt to understand the chemistry of the night. It didn't take long, because the dark hours provided more-than-good fishing in undisturbed surroundings. Setting off in the evening for a night's fishing was like visiting a mysterious island and because I so enjoyed myself I soon became a more or less permanent carp angler. The nights ran into the days and the days merged back into the nights and it was all so agreeable there seemed little point in coming home.

There were still moments of fear, for I would often sit for hours without moving; dozing or sleeping, waiting for a fish. Then a night visitor might approach cautiously, unheeded, and come right up to me. They were simply curious, unsure whether I was *Homo sapiens*, a large otter or a thing from Mars. Once I woke from a dream to find a roebuck staring at me in the face and for a moment I thought the sky had been filled with a gigantic devil's mask. There was a similar encounter with a fox but the most startling of all was when I had a badger actually sniff in my ear.

Some other incidents were more baffling. I have written before about haunted lakes and there is no doubt that some waters have such a powerful atmosphere that, on heavy, overcast nights, it can seem as if the air itself is thickening and forming into fantastic shapes. On one such night, at a carp pool in a Sussex forest, I was fishing, thinking I had the place to myself, (where I fished in the sixties it was more unusual to meet another nocturnal angler than it was to meet a ghost) when someone on the far bank suddenly yelled. It was an awful shriek, as if the man had just sat on a needle. What followed was even more disturbing, for he began running wildly around the bank towards me. I upped and dived into thick bracken, leaving my tackle behind. A vague silhouette came pounding past and ran up the path which led to a distant lane. A few minutes later I heard, far off, the sound of a car roaring away. Gradually all sounds ceased and I emerged from the bracken like a canny pheasant after the beaters had gone by.

For a long time I merely stood still and listened. Had someone been murdered? Should I carry on fishing? Should I go home? I had arrived at the water after dark and the man had probably been there all the time. But had he been fishing, or what?

The pool was only small, perhaps two or three acres. There was no moon above the thick cloud cover. As I stood on the bank the water suddenly appeared to be expanding and enlarging. Then I had a sensation almost as if I was beginning to fall forwards while the pool lipped up round my boots. Was this just a swirling in the brain cells? Or the same thing that had driven the man to panic? A little finger of breeze touched the brambles to one side of me, then brushed past me and streamed away along the water's edge. There were no other sounds; the rest of the forest was intensely still. The pool continued to perplex me in the way it seemed to be outspreading and the thin breeze tangled up with the after-effects of the running man. It didn't need much, just a single crack in the undergrowth opposite, and I was suddenly very frightened. At snail's pace, I retreated as soundlessly as possible back into my hiding place. It was too far to reach my bike in the lane. I would probably never have made it. I just cowered and hoped I wouldn't be noticed.

Dawn came up with frustrating hesitancy and eventually revealed a grey, shrunken-looking pool. The reflections were obscured by an oily surface, but there was nothing mysterious about the scene. At full light I walked round to the far side and found a rod, net and tackle bag. I didn't touch them and they were collected an hour later by the same person, I presume, who had thundered past me in the dark. Though I watched him warily, he looked perfectly normal and untroubled. As he came past me he smiled and said, 'Any luck?' I did not like to ask about the previous night for I thought he might be embarrassed, nor did I mention my own experience, for really nothing had happened. In the bright morning light everything looked ordinary and unambiguous and it didn't seem possible that the small tree-shaded pond could have brewed up such a nightmare. But, at the time, the atmosphere was strange enough to suffocate.

Certain lakes had a reputation for consistent ghostliness while others became haunted simply because of a single bump in the night. I have always enjoyed listening to other people's ghost stories, especially when they concern places I

72

Everything in life began to orbit the still waters.

The original home of the wild carp was the monastery
stew pond, the castle moat, the manor lake; places
mellowed by history.

know. Redmire Pool has been the source of many eerie tales and, just last summer, it was the scene of another extraordinary fright in the night. However, though I like ghost stories, I can't help being sceptical. The night is complex and subtle; it's too simplistic to jump to a supernatural conclusion every time something inexplicable occurs. Usually the haunting is simply in the head as it used to be with me when I was a lad – or is merely a case of mistaken identity. However, it's reassuring to remember the more convincing other-worldly characters, like the Lady of Roffey Park Pond, Redmire's whispering spectre and the phantom horse that canters invisibly round Chiddingstone Castle Lake.

My favourite species, and the one that originally inspired me to become an angler, was the English wild carp (come to think of it, a wild carp is not unlike a barbel in appearance). The original home of the wild carp was the monastery stewpond, the castle moat, the manor lake – places mellowed by history, heavy with atmosphere. It's not surprising that they were the source of so many unearthly stories. But it was the fishing I went for, not the ghosts, and, when I think back, there were very few specific incidents that were truly unaccountable. Mostly it was just the air itself that was strange. The ancient locations made a dramatic setting for a very special kind of angling and the night would just emphasize the drama. But the haunting was instigated mostly by the carp. In fact they could push me towards a mild form of lunacy after several days and nights of tense, expectant waiting with nothing happening. After such a test of faith, it was a necessary anodyne, a blessed relief, to turn to a bright, lively river, where something was always happening. However, as my obsession with carp grew deeper, everything in life began to orbit the still waters and soon the moving waters flowed almost out of my mind.

75

CHAPTER TEN

Henry's Barbel

I have found barbel more mysterious than carp.
Richard Walker (1982)

L eft to me, the world would fall in ruins and I would remain in my chair, enjoying the view. From what I have written it might appear that I live a busy life but, though I spend a large proportion of my time fishing, the greater part is spent on occupations like sitting by my window, watching the grass grow. I like to turn over a few thoughts and contemplate the mood of the day. Often I will imagine myself by a favourite water and recall all its characteristic features and its scents and sounds. In my mind I will stroll along the banks and perhaps a certain area of water will catch my attention. I mark it down for further observation and wander on downstream.

Sometimes these musings will become suddenly inadequate. It won't be good enough merely to think about the river; I have to physically be there. I grab a rod, net and bag and I'm gone within seconds. This happens less frequently than it used to, perhaps only once every four or five days. It is now much more likely that I will not have any say in the matter of where and when I shall go fishing. Someone else will decide for me, subverting me with some enthusiastic fishing talk which concludes with the irresistible invitation to come fishing. Occasionally it is more insistent, as when my good friend Breeks phoned last week to say he had just located a secret dream carp water and I must come and see it *now*.

I don't mind other people choosing my fishing days because I like the elements of chance and surprise. Who knows where I shall be casting tomorrow?

Left to myself I would still be fishing for carp and would probably not even have seen a barbel yet nor fulfilled my childhood dream of fishing the Avon.

76

It was all Henry's fault.

I met Roy Henry Tuckey at Redmire in 1977 and landed his first twenty-pound carp for him. I liked his modest, unassuming nature and his philosophic attitude to life. I also liked the way he suffered a major mental crisis whenever he hooked a big fish and recovered joyfully as soon as it was in the net. We kept in touch after he stopped fishing Redmire and one day he told me a story about a river I had not fished before, the western Rother. I was only mildly interested, for this was the period in the late seventies of my most complete obsession with carp and I would spend ten or twelve weeks of summer by the lakeside. I had not fished a river for years but Henry's tale reminded me of all those places I once knew. It was mere nostalgia for a while but then, during a period of carp inactivity, Henry phoned to say he was going again to the Rother and I would be foolish not to go with him. So I went and we had a memorable day. The river was idyllic: unspoilt, avenued by alders, intimate. It twisted and turned through the beautiful landscape of West Sussex; Elgar country to the north of the South Downs.

It was full of chub, many of them very big, and there were also sea trout, dace and grayling. There were probably other species, but apart from a solitary bream these were the only kinds of fish we saw and cast for. Very quickly the Rother began to fill pages in my angling diary and it became the perfect antidote to the fevers brought on by Redmire and its monster carp.

Henry had also caught barbel in the Thames and spoke glowingly about them. Perhaps we should have a day's barbel fishing? No, I said, I did not know anything about barbel, nor did I think there was time enough to learn, though I had often felt drawn to them. I had always admired the look of them in photographs and illustrations and had avidly read all the well-known barbel literature, but I felt they demanded a long period of study and I did not wish to interrupt my routine so severely.

Henry went off on his own. I went back to Redmire and caught a colossal carp – the biggest ever. Yet, though this event didn't affect my own attitude to carp fishing, it seemed to affect the way I regarded Redmire. Or perhaps it was the way Redmire regarded me, for it is a strange place, with an almost human personality. The mood changed. After I caught the record carp the atmosphere at the pool would often seem to be aloof and remote. And sometimes worse. I used to blame myself, yet, as there is an angel at Redmire there might also be a demon. All kinds of things began to conspire against me. On three different occasions, just as great carp were homing in on my carefully presented bait, a bird flew over their heads and made them bolt for cover; a cast to a fish far out dropped the tackle neatly over the only floating twig in the pool; the wind turned against me; tested knots came mysteriously undone; rats ran off with my bait; a bullock fell in at the wrong moment. Redmire withdrew and I withdrew also, knowing that even though this was just a temporary sulk, I had fished there long enough.

So when, next season, Henry renewed his invitation to come barbel fishing I felt ready for a change of direction and happily accepted.

'Right, then!' he said on the phone. 'See you tomorrow morning at six.'

He banged on my cottage door at that precise hour and, still dreaming, I stumbled downstairs to let him in and make some breakfast. While he had his tea and toast I sorted out some suitable gear. Never having been barbel fishing, I was getting quite excited by the prospect, though I had no idea what I was letting myself in for. Never having seen a barbel before, I was looking forward to making one's acquaintance (it was the only English river fish, apart from the burbot, that I had not actually seen in the flesh). It was 15 July, 1982 – a day I would not forget.

We drove to the Kennet below Newbury, a delightful stretch of river, with the clear water sparkling over clean gravel and rippling between lush weedbeds. The banks were reassuringly overgrown with a mixture of hogweed, nettle, willow-herb, comfrey, rush, ragwort and watermint, all shaded by clumps of willow and alder. The little haven was deserted, which made me feel even more optimistic about the day. Not that I'm truly antisocial – it's just that there is more sense of freedom and peace when you have a river entirely to yourself.

However, as we reached the spot Henry had in mind, my hopes clouded a little. It began to rain. Drizzle I do not mind, but I have never enjoyed, nor caught many fish in, a deluge. Fortunately, it only lasted an hour and afterwards the temperature rose, though the sky remained overcast. It was close and hot, almost tropical. The willows dripped with water; the bankside steamed, filling

the air with delectable, earthy scents. Henry said that conditions couldn't be better.

We fished a long narrow pool bounded by rafts of streamer weed. The water looked dark and promising and only a week before Henry had taken three barbel there. We searched the pool thoroughly from top to bottom and the more familiar I became with its contours the more confident I was that *there*, at a spot where the current curled round a little island of weed, was the precise spot where the barbel lay. A stick of dynamite would have enabled me to prove my point. As it turned out, neither Henry or I had a bite.

I went searching for another place to cast and found an attractive-looking pool where the riverbed shelved steeply after a long stretch of weedy shallows. I had just fished through the first cast when Henry came hurrying down, looking serious.

'Do you know what the time is?' he said. 'Two o'clock. Only half an hour till closing time!'

As usual, there had been no time beforehand to prepare even a flask of tea. We had been fishing intently for six hours without sustenance and so we dumped our tackle and made a run for the local pub.

A break in the middle of a long summer day is to be recommended. I was feeling much more alert and refreshed when we got back to the river at quarter past three. Also, we had missed another heavy downpour; it was just passing away as we pushed through the deep, soaking undergrowth towards our new swims. Henry cast below a tree-hung bend. I concentrated on the weed-fringed shelf and, second cast, hooked a fiercely pulling fish that went deep and far. As I called for Henry to bring the net the hook sprang free and put a curse in the air.

I was using luncheon meat on a size 8 and a single swanshot on the 6-pound line, casting upstream and letting the bait come filtering back through the weed streamers and bumping across the little clear strips of gravel, down to the tail of the pool. After a few minutes I hooked another fish which dived deep into the weed but this time did not come free. It felt, initially, so powerful that I was convinced it had to be a barbel. I called again to Henry, who appeared with the net just as I got the fish up onto the surface. We saw the characteristic up-peaked dorsal and the graceful, golden form.

'Yates has got a barbel!' laughed Henry.

The fish dived, made a bid for the bankside reeds, the rod curving down after it, shaking violently. I brought it back to the surface and Henry blurted out, 'It's a chub!'

I couldn't believe it. We had definitely seen a barbel in the middle of the river and it was certainly on the end of my line. But a big, brassy chub rolled into the landing net and I said it must have changed places with the original fish or else been a master of disguise. It was in perfect condition and weighed almost four pounds, but my suddenly prejudiced eye found it hard to admire.

Henry went back upstream to his original swim. I wandered downstream, where the Kennet flowed quick and shallow round the edge of a picturesque hay meadow. There was a promising-looking pool half-way along this stretch and I fished it for half an hour without so much as a flicker of life on the line. I went on down, passing a swans' nest with seven cygnets, and came to a place where the

80

river narrowed and deepened and the willows leaned almost to the far bank. There was a smooth, dark glide, with a dense bed of weed deflecting the current into the near bank and under a tunnel of drooping willow boughs. Though I had no experience of a barbel's whims, I could not believe that this was anything other than the best barbel swim in the world. Moreover, there were no signs that anyone else had been there before me, reaping the hidden harvest.

The sun finally broke through the cloud over the treeline upstream and each willow glowed like an emerald chandelier. My old cane rod (a Walker-built Avon) looked like a thin beam of gold light against the dark water and as I gazed appreciatively at it the tip jagged over. I missed it. Two casts later, as the bait was trickling down towards a raft of flotsam a few yards below me, there came a tentative vibration up the line which did not develop. Presuming the river had deceived me and that I was in the presence of little chub, I thought of exploring further downstream. But I cast once more and allowed the bait to settle below the flotsam. A few minutes flowed gently past, then the rod curved decisively over and I only really needed to hold firm against the pull. There was a satisfying, solid, deep-hanging resistance and for a few moments it appeared that the fish was not aware of a problem. Then the reel suddenly sang and something powerful swept down the willow tunnel. I stopped it fairly quickly, but the rod's bend – a tight half-circle level with and just above the surface of the river – remained fixed and steady.

Snagged? It dawned on me that this *had* to be a barbel. He was not snagged. He came back upstream grudgingly and then dived again beneath the flotsam. There were numerous submerged branches, but the line somehow missed them all. Keeping the pressure constant, I eventually got the fish to move up into the main pool and it went past with the line cutting a narrow V in the surface and me peering eagerly into the depths after it. But I saw nothing. I thought of shouting for Henry but decided against it. If Henry appeared the fish would probably turn into a seahorse. I had my net and, if this really was my first barbel, I didn't want any distractions.

The fish continued upstream but gentle persuasion brought it round to my way of thinking and it cut along the bank. Just before it reached me it turned away. The rod was still in a half-circle but it began to uncurve by degrees and

81

The only time in my life that I would catch my first barbel.

It was a perfect specimen, a fish of exquisite line.

We took a few photographs then, after a last look,
Henry let it go.

then, suddenly, there it was, just below the surface in mid-river – that absolutely distinctive, elegant shape which was unquestionably a barbel. The sun gleamed on the amber flank and for a moment I was locked in amazement. It was not that it was a huge fish; on the contrary. But I had not seen the like of it before and its appearance had a profound effect, a bit like the time I saw my first carp, when I was five. It gave me a curious feeling of vertigo.

Enough of all this, thought the barbel, and plunged down and away. But he came back and, with the net held steady, I led him towards me. Ultra-careful and not risking unnecessary pressure, I was treating him like nitro-glycerine, though it was I who would have exploded if anything went amiss. The ripples spread as I coaxed him over the mesh and he went in quietly, only objecting when I began to lift. Spray went everywhere.

It could not have come at a better moment. The end of a long day, sunset after

84

rain, the first season out of Redmire, a fine pool on a beautiful river and the only time in my life that I would catch my first barbel.

It was a perfect specimen, a fish of exquisite line, with a gracefully curved back, streamlined head and almost flat underside like a section of an aerofoil. Small, neat scales, large, coral-coloured fins and a gold-rimmed eye, utterly black, like jet. The predominant colour was gold, a transparent gold, as if it was really a silver fish dipped in clarified honey. The gold shaded to olive-green along the back and pearl under the belly and there was a delicate mottling of turquoise on the sides of the head. What I liked best, and which I wasn't prepared for, was the asymmetrical tail, with the upper lobe curved and pointed like a scimitar and the lower lobe rounded like a clover leaf, a tail perfectly adapted for keeping station in a fast current, tight to the riverbed.

I whistled to Henry, who came hurrying down the bank and laughed when he saw what I'd got. We shook hands.

'Congratulations.' he said. 'You are now a bona fide barbel angler'.

It was his barbel, really, for it couldn't have happened without him. We reduced it to 4 pounds 8 ounces, took a few photographs and, after a last look, let it go. It fanned its tail for a minute, then pushed confidently into the main flow.

As we walked back upstream a mist was beginning to form, sliding across the dark surface and spilling over the banks, as if the river was breathing on us.

CHAPTER ELEVEN

River Dream

Of the barbel it is hard to speak with too great praise.
Bernard Venables (1958)

My second barbel, also from the Kennet, weighed over seven pounds and was just so much more petrol poured into an already blazing fire. I was consumed by a new passion, and, though I did not immediately turn my carp rods into bean sticks, the carp themselves began to sink a little lower into the depths. I still went carp fishing, but my thoughts were elsewhere and the intensely static quality of the fishing became almost stifling after the sparkle and animation of the river; with the sensation of the current running up the line and down the rod, there was never a moment by the river that was not alive and vibrant.

Old friends looked at me slightly askance as I over-enthused about my wonderful new discovery. They were suspicious, thinking I had been converted by religious fanatics. New friends just thought I'd gone mad.

'There's a carp a yard and a half long in Redmire,' said Donald Leney, who was once the country's greatest authority on carp and tench. 'That's what you should be fishing for, not those barbel.'

But I had left Redmire behind and was now orbiting a new world.

It was inevitable that I would soon make my first cast into the Hampshire Avon, the country's premier barbel water and the dream river of my childhood. The only real problem was that I did not know any Avon anglers and had no idea where I should go on the river. As usual, I hung about for a bit, waiting for divine intervention. It came in the form of one David Roberts.

I had decided to have a stroll round a local lake and there I met this person who, it transpired, was caught between two pools, a bit like me. He fished for carp, but he also liked barbel angling and could not decide which he preferred. We chatted for hours about the relative merits of our favourite species and tried to decide what it was about them that led us to concentrate all our time and attention on them. David had fished the Avon many times; in fact, he was going again the next day, to a delightful-sounding stretch of river, a ticket water, but one little known to the great majority. Of course I would be going, too.

We went down in David's white pick-up, driving towards Ringwood against a stiff westerly. The forecast was pessimistic, the morning was getting darker, but we did not mind. This was an important day and it could rain elephants if it liked. We turned suddenly onto a little bumpy track which led us out of the hectic 1980s and into a world where the twentieth century had not yet happened.

There were one or two honest, plain cottages, the oak woods were tangled and secretive, there was a prehistoric goat, the hayfields looked as though they had never had a dose of nitrate, the willows were densely clustered on the riverbank and there, shining beyond them, was that great, swift-moving body of water that I had not seen for twenty-four years. Through all that time it was surging on, regardless and eternal, millions of tons of it, bubbling up from the Wiltshire chalk and whispering down to the sea. Even though the morning was grey and breezy, the river didn't look as if it had changed much at all. The long fingers of weed coiled and uncoiled, with that same slightly unreal slow motion, or streamed across the shallows like long loose hair in a wind. The gravel was still golden and even though the light was poor I could see, as we walked along, where it shelved down into deep, enticing-looking pools. We gazed into several barbelish chasms, but didn't stop to drop a bait into them for David was eager to show me his favourite reach of the river, where it curved round the edge of an oak wood, shallow and fast, then deep and steady. The great trees towered over the water, sheltering us from the rain that began falling even before we'd prepared our tackle.

David fished a classic fish-holding spot, where an oak leaned actually into the water, deflecting the current and gathering a raft of flotsam round its roots. He had caught an eight-pounder there on his previous visit. I fished a spot where there was an abrupt depression – a 'pot' – in the riverbed, so that the water suddenly boiled and furled, going from about two to five feet deep. Looking along the surface was like looking at a map, but a coded map. All the contours, the deep weedbeds and the larger, sunken obstructions caused some change in the current and by trying to read the alphabet of ripples and creases I could begin to understand the characteristics of the river. It was much bigger and more powerful than the Kennet, less intimate but more exhilarating, good for a spirit that had begun to silt up in the atmosphere of so many silent, vintage ponds. It was like a crisp, dry white wine after a cellarful of heavy red, or a translucent watercolour after a gallery of dark, mellow oil paintings. Pity about the rain, though. Unlike the first day on the Kennet, this was a cold, persistent, driving rain. It greyed the landscape, flailed the river, got into my sandwiches and eventually down my neck. I sheltered under the trees for a while, thinking it might pass over. It didn't. It drove David from his swim and he came down to say it was time for an early lunch, in the salmon fishers' hut, along the bank.

A salmon fishers' hut is a civilized idea. It would be nice to think there were barbel, roach and chub fishers' huts, but of course only the salmon fisher is deemed worthy of such luxury on the Avon. However, when there are no salmon fishers about, it is not a criminal offence to enter their abodes, so long as you remove your hat, wipe your feet and remember not to extol too highly the virtues of non-salmonids.

We continued fishing into the rain, though it was hopeless and uncomfortable. By the time the storm had finally passed over we were cold and soaked through. David suggested a walk to get the circulation going again, and we went downstream for nearly two miles, pushing through head-high reeds, under lines of willows, along the edges of fields and woods. But it did not seem like two miles, for all the time we were walking we were also peering expectantly into the river, hoping to see a flash of gold, or a dark shape moving across a clear patch of gravel. The light was still dull, though, and all we saw were a few chub and dace swimming near the surface. More encouraging was the surprisingly low population of anglers. We passed only three.

By the time we got back to our rods it was the hour of the fish, that time around sunset when a discernible calm descends over the riverscape and the water assumes its most seductive expression. I began fishing more purposefully, casting across, into the weed streamers, and letting the bait come trundling round and down into the deep pot below. I was using, appropriately, the Mark IV Avon, a rod built by Richard Walker in 1954 and which once defeated a 51 pound carp. The reel was a 1922 wide-drum Allcock 4-inch Aerial, a present from Donald Leney, who used it before the war, fishing for Icelandic salmon. The perfect tackle combination, I felt, for an Avon barbel. (Since then I have concluded that while the Avon is certainly not the best barbel rod in the world, the Aerial is the best reel.) I missed a good, solid bite but had a second chance a few casts later which was a bit like being electrocuted. It was the shock of contact after waiting twenty-four years. The dream river had suddenly become a furious creature which was trying to pull the skin off my bones. I had hooked an Avon barbel.

David arrived on the scene at that moment, having just packed up, fishless. Now he doused me with calming advice, telling me not to worry too much about the weedbeds. But I could not help my anxiety, for the fish had torn unstoppably downstream and I could feel the taut line stretching and creaking through a forest of water buttercup, finally becoming solidly knotted round the stems. I got down below the pivotal point and managed to clear most of the line and get a direct pull to the fish. It would not budge, not even when I slackened off. David marched off into the wood and reappeared brandishing an enormous dead branch with which he tried to drive the fish clear. Good idea, but it did not work and I eventually retrieved a bare hook. There was no point in fishing on so we left the river and its barbel and drowned our sorrows in one of the best pubs in England.

After two days I went back with Henry. During a phone call to him I had described the river and the close encounter and Henry had suddenly become seriously ill and had to take a day off work. (I usually work only on Monday evenings). This time the weather was glorious – warm and windless with a golden sun beaming in a deep blue sky. I led the way into the oak wood and along the high bank to the pool I had fished earlier. It looked a different world. The colours of the riverbank were vividly bright; the Avon had a lustre and clarity that were lacking before; it looked much more like the magically glowing river of my childhood. Henry cast his eye up and downstream, smiled and rubbed his

It looked much more like the magically glowing river of my childhood.

We had sensed an air of expectancy.

hands together. He almost choked when he saw the raft of flotsam where David had fished.

We fished in our respective places, patiently searching, trying to unlock the river's secrets with our special keys. A kingfisher went past, low to the surface, then a buzzard, so high up I could barely see it. At about midday I heard a shout from Henry and ran up the bank to find him tussling with an obviously strong fish. At the edge of a weedbed in midwater a large barbel suddenly appeared, its big pectorals flaring, its tail pushing it steadily upstream against the quick current. Henry kept a grip on it and after it had gone to inspect the bankside reeds it came round, slowly and unspectacularly, into the net. A flawless specimen, absolutely bristling with life, and a much brighter gold than the Kennet fish. It was eight pounds exactly, Henry's second biggest ever. We took its portrait and Henry slipped it gently back.

The afternoon was uneventful, apart from a couple of close shaves with a chub and a missed bite that produced a single barbel scale. We fished on diligently until somewhere around six o'clock, when I realized I was dying of starvation. I had food in my creel and a kettle and stove, but the fishing had so absorbed me that I'd forgotten all about them. It was only the slight blurring of vision, after ten hours, that brought me to my more earthly senses. I put the kettle on and tucked into a magnificent home-made turkey pie. But my enjoyment was marred by a slight sense of urgency. The sun was losing its intensity, sinking lower in the west, and I knew that I should begin fishing more earnestly, that the barbel would be moving soon, nearly as hungry as I. Henry came down when the kettle had boiled, but we drank our tea too quickly. He too had sensed the air of expectancy and we were soon back at our places, casting with baited breath.

I had a powerful belt of a bite, but after a moment of exultation I realized I had hooked a big eel. Eels are the greatest enthusiasts of anything meaty, so I dispensed with Bacon Grill and began fishing with sweetcorn. The light faded and the first stars began to appear in the afterglow. There was a big one above me, a planet, Jupiter, I think, but by gazing up at it I was caught mentally off balance when the rod suddenly jumped in my hands. I struck into thin air. I cast again and the bait was just tripping down into the pot when I heard Henry's

I heard a shout from Henry.

shout echo through the wood. He had gone along to a deep glide which I had pointed out earlier and now I could just hear the words 'Big barbel ... really big fish ... quick.' So I just plonked the rod on the bank and hurried off into the gloaming, muttering, 'You rascal! Just as I was going to crack one out.'

I hadn't realized how dark it had become. Beneath the oaks Henry was no more than a vague ghost, but when I crouched next to him I could see his Avon hooped against the twilight.

'I tell you, Chris,' he said dramatically, 'this is a really big fish.'

And by the way the rod remained acutely, almost statically curved I could tell he wasn't jesting. The tension was full and unwavering, just a throb in the cane every so often, like a tree in a steady gale being hit by an extra gust. For a marvellously charged interval nothing seemed to be happening. The faint blue sur-

face of the river was completely unbroken and the only sounds were the occasional click-click of Henry's reel and his nervous exhalations of breath. Finally, a dark circular ripple spread out below us and we saw a pale barbel-shaped flank rolling in its centre.

Netting it was no easy task, with me hanging onto undergrowth at the bottom of a steep bank while at the same time reaching out over a clotted mass of marginal weeds. After one near-perilous mistake, I got the fish between the arms of the net and heaved it safely up. A beauty; an astounding beauty. It looked immense in the half-dark and we guessed it must be almost ten pounds. We hurried back to my creel where, by matchlight, we weighed Henry's best barbel at nine and three-quarter pounds.

As I shook him by the hand there was a sound of music next to me. *Graaaaark*! It was the familiar voice of Leney's old Aerial. I pounced onto the rod, struck and felt that solid but vibrant barbelish resistance. 'Yes!' I said. It was a relief as much as anything to have the rod plunging and heaving and to know that, after the long day, I'd got something worthwhile, especially having seen Henry's grand fish. The reel sang out again and I ran downstream round a

A fish that perfectly expressed the wild nature of its environment.

clump of reeds, to the clear stretch of bank immediately over the deep water. There I could get right on top of the barbel and hold it clear of the weeds.

Henry released his fish and came down with the net. I hung on, but made little impression on my adversary. It seemed completely indifferent to my superb playing technique and was just trying to decide which was the most devastating way to smash me up. But it didn't leave the deep hole and I gradually pressured it up to the surface. It lashed out and again we saw dark ripples spreading across the reflected twilight. The splash sounded shockingly loud in the silence and I wondered whether this was another whopper. Down it went again and being directly above it I could feel every swipe of its tail, every swerve and roll. There was a nasty moment of blocked communication when, after an unexpected downstream charge, the line caught suddenly in the weeds, but I swung the rod over to my left and eased it free.

Again, netting was problematic, with a marshy, deceptive bit of bank and marginal weed. Stumbling, splashing and flooding his boots, Henry finally got the fish, but as he backed through the marsh the net frame collapsed and he fell over. Wonderful entertainment. Even Henry laughed. My first Avon barbel, at six and three quarter pounds, looked almost diminutive after Henry's specimen, but even in the faint light I couldn't but admire the darkly glowing sabre-like form, a fish which by its shape perfectly expressed the wild nature of its environment.

It seemed the perfect culmination to the dream I'd been quietly nursing since childhood and which now had led me back to the Avon, where we had caught magical fish on a still, luminous evening.

We packed up in a bit of a daze, walked out of the wood and came into a field white with glowing mist. The moon was hanging in the southern sky and the river, curving beneath it, was full of splintered gold.

CHAPTER TWELVE

Anniversary Carp

T he dawn was red, yet the shepherd's warning was unfounded. By the time the mist had cleared the sun was really hot and there wasn't a cloud in the sky.

I drove down to the pond at 11.30 and there was an indefinable blue haze hanging over everything. Perfect September. I walked all round the tree-lined banks, searching for carp. As usual, there was no one else there and I had the choice of the best pitches. Carp were moving in the corner by the overspill and I watched the water slowly furl and bulge as they patrolled through the lily pads.

Despite the ascendancy of the barbel, on that day I could not possibly fish for anything but carp. Not only was it the thirtieth anniversary of Richard Walker's historic record carp; I had also just received a letter from him saying that, yes, he would be delighted to become president of the Golden Scale Club. Not only that, the club – of which I am secretary – had just got hold of the very rod with which Richard subdued his famous fish. Since September 1952 this original Mark IV had been hanging, admired but unused, in a glass case. But now was the day when, at last, it could flex its fibres again at a carp pool. Excalibur had risen once more. Richard had used the Mark IV, a Mitchell 300 loaded with 12-pound braided line and an Allcock Model Perfect hook, size 6. In keeping with tradition I coupled the rod to the appropriate reel, having loaded it with 12-pound braided line. But I had no more Model Perfect hooks and so made do with a Mustad. The bait Richard had fished with was bread, but, while the carp in his water had not seen much bread before and soon got a taste for it, the carp in my pond were embarrassed to even look at the stuff. They knew all about its more dubious qualities and were much happier eating peanuts, especially maple-flavoured peanuts.

Instead of fishing by the overspill, I waded out through the reeds so that I could drop a bait in a narrow strip of open water between the reeds and the dense lily bed. Departing again from tradition I also used a little cork-bodied quill. I wanted to have an early indication of my bite so that I could at least raise a fish into midwater before it barged through the lilies.

It seemed too hot and airless. The sun was beating, or rather pouring, a liquid heat straight down on me, yet, after two hours, just as I was thinking of moving back into the shade, a carp cruised towards the float and descended beneath it. Bubbles appeared on the surface as it found the free scattering of nuts. I did not actually see the float disappear; I was watching the bubbles and suddenly realized it wasn't there any more. But I struck at nothing and a big, slow wave surged off under the pads. At least it proved they were feeding. So I left my gear for a while and went off to sit under the trees on the dam while I had my beer and sandwiches. As I ate, I could see the fish slowly parading through the lilies. Occasionally a great back would rise very gradually through the surface film and gleam quite brightly in the sunlight. The very soft intermittent breeze, which might have been the result of the heat mixing with the cool of the surrounding woods, was just enough to stop the carp from lying absolutely doggo. With each little draught the fish stirred slightly. Across the three or four acres of open water there were no signs of fish. They had all congregated under their parasols.

Refreshed and rested, I went back into the reeds, baited with two peanuts and dropped the tackle just a yard short of the pads. A carp drifted nearby, coming to the edge of the pads but then suddenly turning back into them. He looked big.

Another fish ghosted serenely past and then another, moving down towards the dam. The perspiration prickled on my forehead.

At mid-afternoon a large carp cruised slowly in from my right, approaching cautiously between the dinnerplate-sized leaves, then emerging from their shade and sinking down not far from the float. I was ready – even expecting it. Without any hesitation or dithering the quill slid straight under and I stuck to the left against the direction it was heading. *Voosh*! There was a great erupting swirl and all the pads rose and fell like a flotilla of rafts on a tidal wave. Then a

An indefinable blue haze hung over the lake.

Walker's old rod had stood the test of time.

deep furrow opened up in the surface as the fish ploughed through the lily bed from right to left.

Excalibur took on its battle curve and the reel let out a prolonged squeal. The carp, pulling like a horse, curved round so that the line described a half-circle through the pads. They swayed and jostled as the fish drove down. The water heaved. I tightened, felt him turn and come back a few yards. But then he surged away again and there was a terrible sensation of line stretching and snagging against tough stems. I winced and there was a twang and jolt as a pad suddenly flicked like a butterfly into the air. I thought for a moment that the hook had gone, but the living resistance was still there and the old rod was beginning to win against it. The carp came wallowing and churning back to the

100

point on the edge of the lilies where the line slanted into them. For a tense moment the fish became lodged solid, but then he rolled over, shook himself free, and in a moment the torn-up leaves were all behind him and the line was cutting wonderfully through open water.

The net was ready, but I knew the fish was not going to come straight over it. The tackle was powerful, though, and I was able to hold him back from the various sanctuaries which surrounded us – the lilies, the reeds and several submerged branches. He looked a grand fish, perhaps twenty pounds and fully scaled. Darkly he loomed towards me but then caught me by surprise by suddenly rocketing into the reeds on my left. The stems waved and danced as I reached forward and persuaded him back into the clear. He rolled and made a jab for the pads but, after taking a few yards of line, was eased round in a circle. He surfaced, looking tired, though there was not so much exhaustion as resignation in his gradual surrender. I craned over the reeds with the net, waited until he was right up over the frame, then lifted. The water exploded and I felt the handle pulling viciously as he drove against the mesh. But I held on tight and eventually he calmed down. He was too heavy to lift over the reedbed and I had to unscrew the handle, get hold of the frame and heave. The weight was intensely satisfying and the beauty of the thing I'd caught made me burst into song.

It was a lovely, burnished-gold-common carp of twenty and a quarter pounds. The old rod had stood the test of time and I went home to write a letter of appreciation to its maker.

*A lovely, burnished gold common carp of twenty and a
quarter pounds.*

CHAPTER THIRTEEN

The Sound of the Weir

This fish is of a fine cast and handsome shape … he loves to live in very swift
streams or where it is gravelly or on Piles about Weirs or Floodgates or Bridges,
that the water be not able, be it ever so swift, to force him from the place which he
seems to contend for …

Izaak Walton on the barbel (1653)

Through the high summer and autumn of my first year's barbel fishing I visited the Avon whenever I possibly could, even though it was almost seventy miles from home. I enjoyed myself immensely, happy with the realization that, having got into my dreams, the river was now getting under my skin. Yet after that promising start with Henry I caught only one more barbel in half a dozen trips. I did not care; fishing can be wonderful, even without fish, and I was learning all the time. Also, the more I didn't catch barbel the more I wanted one. It was like making an investment, increasing my interest rate while I waited for an extravagant moment when I could withdraw everything in one glorious go.

The Avon confirmed me as a barbel addict and also won my love. I thought it the most beautiful river I had ever fished. Even though it was often perplexing and baffling, that very mystery together with its appearance and powerful character won me over completely.

In early October a wonderful person called Boris 'Bob' Burchett, hearing that I'd fallen under the river's spell, invited me to fish a little stretch near Burgate where he and his friends were sometimes given leave to go. There, he said, were barbel big enough to cure even an obsession like mine.

I was round at Boris's house at six the next morning and we drove down to the Avon in a large estate car, accompanied by a boffin, a colonel and a man called

103

Ferret. They seemed a decent enough bunch and were as joyful as I about going fishing, even though it was pouring with rain. It rained all day.

The Colonel kindly walked me along the entire fishery and pointed out all the best barbel-holding pools. Being an army man, he kept his obvious enthusiasm in check, but there was an almost manic gleam in his eyes when he described how, on his last visit, he had dismissed a certain pool as unfishable only to have a friend fish the swim after him and bag an eleven-pounder.

It says a lot for their characters that, despite absolutely atrocious weather, the anglers were still cheerful at the end of the day. They had not drunk much ale at the pub at lunch time, they had not caught any fish; they simply valued their time by the river. They did not even mind the fact that I *did* catch a fish – the only one of the day. It was a chub which might have weighed a pound.

'Come again in November,' they said.

We drove down on the eleventh day of that month. The weather was soft and still and as we travelled across the New Forest a crescent moon appeared in the dawn sky. The road led steeply into the Avon valley and we glimpsed the river, iron grey in the early light. After days of rain it was high, coloured and flowing strongly – perfect conditions, what with the mild weather, for a late-autumn barbel.

Boris and Ferret went down to fish a deep pool by a suspension bridge. I walked upstream to the main weir. The sun rose out of the dawn mist and the water began to glow. I found a deep, steady back-flow and began to float-fish, using my newly acquired Wallis Wizard – a lovely old piece of cane, which, in its original pre-war version, was the first Avon rod to be commercially produced.

I missed the first bite, but made contact the very next cast. The fish was enormous – for a gudgeon. It even put a bend in the rod. I caught another within ten minutes. It took a whole lobworm. The two of them must have weighed almost quarter of a pound.

Taking off the float, I added another swanshot to the line and moved up next to the weir lasher. A weir pool is a classic setting for barbel fishing. The river surges over the sill, roaring as it goes. The clouds of bubbles, dark whorls and furls in the surface completely obscure the view into the depths, yet the angler can easily imagine the shadowy forms of barbel down there, holding station in

104

the powerful current. The turbulent water seethes across them, but they maintain their position without effort.

I flicked a bait alongside the weir apron and as it swung round and settled in a quiet slack I felt sure the barbel were close by – perhaps not there in the main current, considering the extra volume of water, but they were near. I fished both sides of the weir, searching the slack and the smooth flow along the edge of the white apron. However, apart from a few tweaks and knocks – probably gudgeon again – there was no response.

As usual the hours sped by and it was lunch time before I'd really got the feel of the water. There was a pub close by the river, but I was too eager to get back to the weir to really enjoy my repast. What made it worse was when the bailiff strode in for his midday pint and, hearing of my deep desire for barbel, came over and whispered: 'The weir's the place for you, my boy.'

I refused a second beer and hurried back to the river. Coming along the bank I passed a deep slack that suddenly attracted my attention. I hesitated, then dumped my gear and began to fish. Just a couple of casts, I told myself, yet I

A weirpool is the classic setting for barbel fishing.

stayed there till sunset, all the while expecting the lightning-stroke bite of a barbel. I was sure my instincts had not deceived me, yet there was not a tremor of interest from a fish. The sun had gone down, the light was fading and all the while I was conscious of the distant, insistent sound of the weir. I'd wasted valuable time and I hastily gathered my creel and net and quickly marched up river. There was another, unknown angler in the slack corner of the east bank which was the spot I had intended to fish, so I went across the weir hatches to the opposite side and began fishing a gentle back-flow which ran alongside a bed of withered sedge. I had exhausted my supply of lobworms and only had a few chunks of luncheon meat left, but I was unconcerned. In my limited experience of barbel fishing I had learnt that, when the fish suddenly demystify themselves, one bite is all you need. I cast so that the simple two-shot leger landed along the bank towards the weir sill, only a yard from the half-submerged reeds.

The twilight sank and the clouds drifted away, revealing the first stars. Soon all I could see of the weir was the trail of foam like a white banner furling in the wind. The roaring of the water seemed to increase in volume as night came on. I felt the feeblest vibration running down the rod. Was there a fish on the bait? Then it stopped and I wondered whether I should have tried striking.

The angler who had been fishing the other bank packed up and I saw his silhouette coming across the hatches. He carefully picked his way round to where I was sitting and asked how I was faring. His name was Brian Shaw and he was the stockman on the local farm. He told me that he fished the river regularly, mostly for barbel, but also for salmon, chub and roach, and he had landed some splendid fish.

I was just going to ask him whether he rated my chances when the tip of the Wizard wrenched over. It was impossible to miss, yet I am sometimes capable of the impossible. I missed another, more tentative bite a few minutes later. Brian was less concerned than I.

'Don't worry,' he said. 'I know you're going to get one.'

We continued our conversation. Brian spoke sadly of the general decline of the Avon and said how, years before, he could walk those banks and see great shoals of roach, dace and chub, all gone now.

'The water authority tells us the fish are still there, but I ask them to come

107

along and show me where.'

He blamed the trout farms, with all the hundreds of tons of raw fish dung pouring into the river and, even worse, the toxic chemicals and antibiotics the breeders use to control disease. The water authority's weed-cutting policy also incurred his wrath.

'Calamitous! Taking away the fishes' larder and sanctuary all at the same time.'

Yet somehow his favourite, the barbel, was still flourishing.

While Brian was talking I missed three more bites and so used up the last of my bait. I had just resigned myself to another blank when a fresh can of bait miraculously appeared. My new friend for life had a spare tin in his bag.

'You must get one now,' he said, and of course I would, even if I had to sit there till Christmas.

There was another edgy sort of pull which did not come to anything. Then I rebaited, stood up and made a careful cast inches from the stonework at the side of the lasher. As I was sitting down there was a beautiful decisive heave which even I could not miss (I like to think all those previous bites were from bootlace eels.)

The reel sang out even above the voice of the weir as a big fish moved out of the enclosed corner and rushed headlong down the main surge.

'That's a good fish,' said Brian. 'Could be a double.'

'It's probably just a salmon,' I said.

In a light evening breeze we could faintly hear the taut line whining like a heartbroken cat. I followed the fish's direction by watching the Wizard as it swung against the stars. For the first time I could use the extra stiffness in the butt and every fibre in the old rod tightened like steel. It was quite obviously a barbel; no other fish maintains its depth so determinedly, keeping irresistibly low to the riverbed and arguing obstinately over every inch of line.

I was only using 5-pound line so I could not afford to be heavy-handed, yet after a few minutes I managed to coax the fish to the surface, where it plunged heavily, breaking the dark water with an even darker swirl. I tried to keep him on top but he turned and dived with tremendous force, heading far out across the pool and causing my gillie to jump up and warn me about the rocks and

boulders under the weir sill.

The barbel stopped and I presumed he was simply hanging steady before changing direction, but then I realized that he had buried into weed, or clamped down behind a rock. No, it was worse. The line was dead. He was gone. I was sure of it.

'Don't pull!' said Brian. 'He's still there. He'll come in the end.'

I kept the rod gently curved, eased it this way and that, but all to no avail and I lamented that my biggest barbel had joined the list of the lost.

Then, so gradually that I at first hardly noticed, the pressure began to change and ease and a great weight rose up and swept downstream with the flow. For a moment I thought it was just a loose clot of weed or a branch but then there was a terrific thump on the rod and I knew the world was whole again. With the line whining and singing I persuaded the fish round and back into the quieter water. Then he surfaced and we saw him for the first time – a vague, pale, wondrous shape on the black waters. Descending once more, he speared himself towards the half-drowned sedges and I gave the tackle as much as I dared to keep him clear of them. Back he came, surfacing closer this time.

'He's a really good fish,' said Brian.

Any barbel was a really good fish, but this one looked phenomenal. He righted himself, turned, then came back towards the outreaching net. Gently, gently, as smooth as you can. A little more pressure. The rod lifted a little higher. And then the net was rising.

'Oh yes!' said Brian. 'He's double figures all right!'

Great exultation as we laid the fabulous creature onto the grass, the most impressive-looking fish I had seen in years. Though it was dark and we had no lamp, I could see it in every detail, as if I had suddenly been gifted with owl vision. Or was it the fish actually glowing? I noted the flawless scaling, the wing-like pectorals and the larger-than-handspan tail. He was big, but not old; a prince of the river. I whispered salutations and apologies to him and shook him gently by the fin; then I thanked Brian and he said we should get the spring balance out, even though he agreed that it was rather irreverent. But of course we weighed him as accurately as possible, in flickering matchlight, and though I refused to look at the pointer Brian assured me that it hung steady at ten pounds six ounces.

I carried the fish back to the water's edge and held it a while on the surface, letting the final image of it swim away into my head....

The most impressive looking fish I had seen in years.

CHAPTER FOURTEEN

Canes and Pins

I live in an old flint cottage which is half-timbered with split-cane rods. I am admiring my favourites as I write: the delectable little $10^{1}/_{2}$-foot Allcock Lucky Strike, straight as a needle after thirty years and countless big fish; the old reliable Wallis Wizard, which mastered another ten-pound barbel recently; a superb, steely, original James Avocet; a Hardy Wanless, at 7 feet the perfect bush rod for carp and chub; a quick-tipped pre-war 14-foot Hardy Thames Style; *the* Mark IV Avon; and a powerful 12-foot Chapman Hunter, which was foolishly lent to me by the rod maker Edward Barder (he may not get it back). Then there are the fly rods.

I deplore the acquisitiveness of modern society and I have never really understood how people can passionately collect things like stamps and old bottles. But here I sit, surrounded by bits of vintage cane, and I know there are several corners in this house that have yet to receive their proper quota. I reassure the lovely person who sometimes threatens these rods with a Hoover that I have not acquired them simply because I like the look of them; they are all for use. I *need* them. I must have them.

It wasn't always like this. I began with a length of whole cane, stolen from the garden, and only after several years did I reach that happy position in life when I owned a real, serious fisherman's rod like the ones in the catalogue, endorsed by famous names. Eventually I had a choice of two rods – one long and slickly finished, which I was proud to use, the other short and tatty and which caught all the fish. I would handle the rods in the local tackle shop and, while I was interested in them all, there were always one or two that would have a special quality, a distinctive feel. The craftsmanship, the perfect taper, the seasoning of the

112

It's difficult finding a tackle shop nowadays that will give you credit.

canes before they were split, the way the cane actually grew, the time it was cut and the nature of the soil and rainfall and air where it grew – all these things were important in the creation of a truly classic rod. And yet you could handle dozens of rods that met all these particulars and only one would have that extraordinary feel, which is almost like a life in itself.

'Careful with that Hardy, son, it's fifteen guineas.'

A lovely-looking rod, beautifully finished. The envy of any roach angler you were likely to meet on the Mole. But it didn't have the feel. I put it back carefully in the rack and took out an inexpensive Allcock Record Breaker (I say inexpensive, but it would still have cost six months' pocket money). Ten and a half feet, three-piece split cane, plainly whipped and finished, with a crisp, sensitive action. It had the feel. There was an elegant 12-footer by Auger which certainly had it, but the 11-footer by the same firm was far too wobbly. I liked the action of a James Avocet, with a whole-cane butt, and though the Kennet Perfection was a bit floppy I was attracted by the dense intermediate whippings. Last of all I waggled the James Mark IV Avon. I had a ten-shilling deposit on that rod and one day it would be mine. Ten feet and two-piece with a slow, easy action and a particular quality that I found very appealing. It had magic but it did not have the feel I am trying to describe. It would be hard to precisely convey the Avon's feel. Vague, I suppose, but with hidden power. Rods which had a balanced steely sensitivity and would give you tremendous confidence in a specific kind of fishing, these are the instruments I am talking about. However, when you could handle several rods of similar design and dimensions and only one had this unique characteristic, it makes cane waggling sound like the tactile equivalent of wine tasting. Moreover, it was all academic, for when I finally got enough pennies for my Avon I could still make a red-letter day out of a one-pound chub.

In the mid-1960s hollow fibreglass rods began to appear and, like everyone else, I was curious. Hollow glass rods had a nice smooth, fluid action, they were nearly all the same jaundiced colour and if you accidentally put your foot on one it made a lovely squashy noise, as if you'd stood on an egg. My first real carp rod was hollow glass but my Avon outfished it every time, even when I put two identical baits within a yard of each other. The magic of the Avon always won over the soulless efficiency of the carp rod – which, of course, doesn't make

Cane and pin in action on a Kennet weirpool.

sense, except to a cane man. Eventually a cow trod on the glass rod and it looked like a reed stem at the end of winter.

Then, ten years later, carbon fibre appeared. Carbon rods were very expensive, much finer in diameter than either cane or glass, extremely light and with a kind of contradictory action which was stiffly pliant. Very precise, very sharp and, like the glass rods, every one machine-made. Again, you had to be extra careful you didn't squash them underfoot or in a car door. But the carbon rod's special appeal lay in its ability to surprise. It gave such an impression of super-efficiency that it always came as a bit of a shock when, as you applied that steely power to keep a big fish from the weeds, there was a sharp crack and you were left holding nothing but the cork handle. This unpredictability gave fishing a new, exciting dimension. You never knew when or if or where along the rod the break would occur. It kept you on your toes and gave added drama to every big fish you hooked.

Of course there are thousands of carbon rods still fishing today, all with impeccable, courageous characters. But their owners must not forget that an inherent flaw may be hidden somewhere in those fibres and that, at a psychologically critical moment, that flaw may become apparent and another section of brittle, broken rod will go sliding down the line.

Now, with craftsman-built cane.... But no, I think I've said enough.

Reels are a slightly different kettle of fish. My rod prejudice could be merely a matter of nostalgia, but any angler worth his salt knows that, for river fishing, there is no reel better than a good centrepin. Fixed-spool reels have their place, especially if they are a Hardy Altex, but for most kinds of river fishing the centrepin is supreme. The advantages when trotting a float are obvious, but the rolling leger is my favourite method and here the centrepin is again superior. There are no fiddly pauses while you open the pick-up and then close it again; it is all one fluid action with the rhythm of casting, following through and retrieving. Naturally, it is not so fluid if suddenly your faultless Wallis cast develops a birdsnest, but practice makes perfect, or so I am told.

When I began fishing I used a horrid little blue tinplate 'centrepin'. I didn't know it was horrid because everyone else on the village pond had one exactly the same, though in different colours, and we all believed you couldn't possibly use anything else. But then a newcomer appeared with a strange revolutionary device on his rod called an Intrepid De-Luxe. With this engine he could cast to the island every time. It was the first fixed-spool we had ever seen. The newcomer could reach fish that had always been out of bounds to us and he had a netful of perch and gudgeon within the hour. We were horrified, not because we thought he had an unfair advantage. Small boys are not prey to fundamentalist strictures. We were shocked because *we* hadn't got a De-Luxe.

Perhaps the newcomer was an intrepid missionary, come to convert us from our heathen ways. We never saw him again, but the firm profited from his visit. After the De-Luxe I progressed to the connoisseur's Elite, the 'ultimate in fixed-spool reels'. After four years it disintegrated while I was playing a nine-pound carp, but by then it was obsolete because the Japanese had invaded.

I caught my first twenty-pounder using a Shakespeare Europa, and that reel is still going, even though a 'friend' called Jasper stole it from me years ago. Mitchell 300s were a carp angler's standard issue, but, though I used them, I preferred the more eccentric and perfectly reliable Allcock Ambidex. I caught my two biggest carp using the A.A., but through all my years of carp fishing I preferred the 'pin' if I could get away with using it. There is nothing like playing a twenty-pound carp on a centrepin: its movements and its strength are not absorbed through the gears; you are directly in contact. Apart from a small-diameter Aerial, I never possessed any 'quality' reels, but found my old Strike-rights and Grice and Youngs perfectly adequate, especially for margin fishing. Nowadays, on the rivers, I am a bit more particular. My carp reels are rather clumsy and heavy for trotting and trundling and, as I said elsewhere, the wide-drum four-inch Allcock Aerial is unsurpassed. I now have several other fine centrepins, but none of them suit me as well as this wonderful seventy-year-old winch. With it I can cast off the drum thirty yards, which is far enough for most situations. However, I confess I am at the mercy of the wind, for if it is blowing left to right I am scuppered and my casting distance halved. If you have not attempted the Wallis or Nottingham cast I cannot explain why. It's all to do with spin, thumb control and the size of the line bow. Also, with me, it's to do with cack-handedness, but I am working on that.

I can cast almost as far with a reel that is not an antique, is a really sweet winch and is still manufactured today. I am talking here about an item of modern, up-to-date equipment that I, a rigid traditionalist, approve of – The Swallow centrepin. And I promise this has nothing whatsoever to do with the fact that the man who makes these reels lives opposite a very good Avon barbel swim, only two hundred yards from an oak-beamed pub.

I often wonder what the Golden Scale Club's spiritual president, Isaak Walton, would have said about the limitless choice of reels available to today's angler. The ultrasophisticated fixed-spools, which look as though they have fallen off the back of a starship, would probably have rendered him speechless. But then even the first rudimentary reels were beyond him. He never used one and, in the only passage in the *Compleat Angler* to refer to them, he is ultimately lost for words:

Note also that many used to fish for a Salmon with a ring of wire on the top of their Rod, through which the Line may run.... And to that end, some use a wheel about the middle of the Rod, or near their hand, which is to be observed better by seeing one of them, than by a large demonstration of words.

CHAPTER FIFTEEN

The Time of My Life

I had a health problem and having decided that my entire system had been suffering from a chronic lack of barbel and river water I realized that I would have to seek earnestly for a cure. For too many years I had been gradually and insidiously silting up on the banks of various, admittedly lovely, carp ponds. Now I would have to move house and live by the Avon.

Years ago I was told by some crotchety, pessimistic rationalist that it was dangerous to let your desires and compulsions rule your life.

'The heart must not rule the head. Logic will always triumph. Emotional responses are a sign of weakness. Those who think that life comes before work will not survive these times.' Etc., etc.

Even when I was young and more impressionable, such arguments were hardly convincing. I reasoned that most people didn't have much choice in the matter, having too early in their lives allowed the 'system' to make all the important decisions. They had been denied all the opportunities I had enjoyed and so had not become mesmerized by water, but they had become mesmerized by one of society's great illusions and so needed lots of money to buy all the inessential things that they were offered, like videos, microwave ovens, satellite dishes, fast cars, jacuzzis, carbon rods. To make this money they sacrificed all their time, following the established rule that time is money. But time is life and if everyone accepted this the system would collapse. People would not need to spend their lives making money to buy unnecessary gadgets and could therefore go a-fishing more often. The firms who made the gadgets would all go bankrupt and so the employees could also spend more time on the bankside. Everyone would demand less and live more simply, in the spirit of Isaak; no one would be able to afford petrol and the motorways could be turned into canals and stocked with carp. The world could become less frantic, less noisy, more civilized and leisurely. We would all go fishing on bicycles and everyone would be happy.

I had, as you might guess, a fairly basic academic education. What, I wondered, were they trying to teach me? What did they expect me to become? Would their teaching assist me in the world? Was it essential to understand the trade relationships between Britain and Bolivia? The date of Henry VIII's third marriage? Or the theories of Pythagoras? I would spend hours gazing vacuously out of the window. And, if it was a fine day and I was in the school's east wing, I would be able to see the course of a little brook, indicated by a line of hawthorns and a few flashes of sunlit water. I would then allow my thoughts to float away downstream, and though my reverie would occasionally be interrupted by a piece of well aimed chalk or a thump on the back of the head I might be able to float on the brook all the way down to the Thames, where I could sink into the depths and swim along with the roach and bream shoals till the end of the lesson. Sometimes this psychological exit wouldn't be good enough and, though I should be ashamed to confess it, I would *physically* escape.

There was a hole under the fence behind the bicycle sheds and if you could reach it without being seen from the staff room or the maths room you were a free man. It was all a matter of timing, though in my case I don't think this mattered much at all. Had a star pupil been caught making an escape attempt he would have been dragged back in chains and given a dressing down in front of the whole school. But had I been spotted I rather think my teachers would have turned a blind eye, glad to be rid of me – though perhaps this is being unfair to my dear English and Art tutors, whose language I think I understood. Once through the hole in the wire you had to crawl to the elms on the far side of the field. It was not grazed or cut for hay and, in the summer at least, there was a kind of rudimentary tunnel burrowed through the long grass by the small and happy band of escapees who regularly came that way. (No good if you suffered from hay fever.) Once under the elms you could creep behind a hedgerow and so down to the stream. There you could spend your freedom, swinging across the water on a rope we had tied to an overhanging tree or trying to catch minnows and bullheads with your hands.

It was during one of these excursions, sitting on the banks of the stream and watching the water, that I decided that my life must always be like this. It was a wonderful feeling to be lounging about in the sun, swinging in the air or catching fish while your pals sweated it out in the science room less than a mile away. Of course I felt sorry for them, but I would have been more sorry if I had been with them. Before anyone else made any decisions for me, I vowed that I must find a way to exist and yet also be free to sit by the waterside whenever I wished. Watching the stream ripple past was a lesson in itself. I could enjoy its cheerful appearance, chase its cheerful inhabitants, swing over it with cheerful abandon, become part of its existence. But if I wasn't there, the brook carried on cheerfully without me. Life did just the same. If you had no desire to plunge in and

121

A summer expedition to Redmire.

We did not buck up or buckle down, life was not compromised.

The author and the Gaffer on the riverside.

become part of it, it went on without you and you ended up spending your afternoons in the science room.

When I was fifteen I took one O'level exam, in Art, and then spent the next six years at art school. Happy days. I took a great deal of time to compile a folio of rather hurried sketches of all my favourite waters. I devoted an entire term to my illustrated 'thesis' on an obsessive quest for a carp.

I made a 16mm film, which necessitated several days and nights on the banks of a particularly beautiful Sussex carp lake. Mainly because of the photographic tutor, Roy Sims, who gave me an encouraging shove at a strategic moment, I ended up with letters after my name. And then, thanks to the faith and generosity of my wonderful parents, I used home as base camp for the next few years, wintering there while taking on photographic commissions (record and book covers were my bread and butter) and setting out on expeditions in the summer

124

to all the most important places in the world – Milton Mount, New Pond, Titmus Lake, Roffey Park, Furnace Lake, the Borrick Derg, Sheepwash, Redmire.

In 1974 I was checked in mid-cast by a striking-looking brown-eyed girl who caused an earthquake even more severe than the one which destroyed my roach fishing. Worlds collided, carp lakes dried up, fish evaporated, I lost the top joint of my Mark IV Avon, spring in Paris was enchanting. When the universe re-formed I found myself in paradise, somewhere near Haslemere. We were living in a cottage in a wood, surrounded by carp lakes, sharing our garden with badgers, grass snakes, roe deer and purple emperors. Pity about the mortgage.

The years floated by. We did not buck up or buckle down; life was not compromised, though this sometimes meant penury. And when I thought that it would be good for my health to be nearer the Avon, the Gaffer was pleased for she liked the downland country of Cranborne Chase, to the west of the river. Moreover, we both agreed that, while our cottage was a barn of pleasant memories, the shadow of the developer was looming over the local village, destroying the atmosphere and character of the place.

I would miss the lakes of the Haslemere Angling Society, I would miss the fauna of our wood, I would sorely miss the little Sussex Rother; I would miss Derek at the tackle shop and Patrick at Waggoner's Wells; but most of all I would miss Donald Leney, at whose rambling fifteenth-century house I spent many happy tea times, discussing Life on Earth and Life in Water.

We moved to Cranborne Chase in the winter of '86 and almost immediately England was struck by the grandest blizzard of the decade. We were snow-bound. Lakes froze, the river turned black with cold and icicles festooned the weirs. I didn't go fishing for weeks....

125

Lakes froze, the river turned black and icicles festooned the weirs.

CHAPTER SIXTEEN

Royalty Days

~

R ichard Walker warned me about the Royalty. 'It can be like a circus,' he said, 'but the barbel fishing is wonderful.'

All the photographs I had ever seen of it put me off. Compared with the rest of the Avon, the Royalty Fishery looked bleak and uninspiring: the eastern skyline wired across with pylons; the west bank nudged by the buildings, warehouses and bustle of Christchurch. Also, some of the stories I heard were discouraging: how there were sometimes queues for a day ticket and how you needed gallons of maggots to get the barbel feeding. However, a series of blank days on the middle river plus a meeting with a Christchurch native persuaded me that I should at least have an exploratory cast there.

I went down one mild winter weekend. I didn't have to queue to buy our tickets and Graham at the tackle shop said I wouldn't need a gallon of maggots. Though the surroundings were not wonderful and there were dozens of anglers along the banks, the river possessed such a variety of pools, bends, deeps, shallows and glides that it was hard to decide where to fish. My immediate impression was that the Royalty was much more intimate than I had expected – smaller and more characterful.

I only caught one barbel, a $3^{1}/_{2}$-pounder, but I also caught the spirit of the place and I would have to come back.

I told Ferret what I had discovered and he came down with me on the next visit. Ferret – whom I met on the road to Burgate and who had become a good friend – also has barbel in his blood and is as compulsive about his fishing as I am. We chose a weekday and were delighted to find we had the entire Royalty to ourselves. Even though the weather conditions were not ideal – a bitterly cold

wind and a bright sky – Ferret caught a brace (five and six pounds) and, scaling down to light tackle because I couldn't get a bite, I had an epic battle with a barbel of $5^3/_4$ pounds. Ferret was impressed; I was encouraged enough to return, on my own, the following Monday.

It had rained continually and tumultuously for three days and it was still raining when I loaded my gear into my old van on Monday morning. For ten minutes I sat behind the steering wheel trying to decide whether to start the engine. I guessed it was silly to go to the barbel when, judging by the volume of water falling over my head, the barbel would soon be coming to me. It was crazy to even contemplate fishing on such a day. But, even though it took ten minutes, the rational arguments were inevitably crushed and away I went along roads which ran like rivers.

Graham looked up from his coffee and blinked in astonishment when I burst, dripping wet, into his tackle shop and asked for a Royalty ticket. (I'd got soaked running the fifty yards from my van to his door.)

'Didn't expect to see anyone fishing today,' he said. 'River's up. Still rising. If you've got an aqualung you might do well.'

The fields along the east bank were flooded but I was going to fish the House Pool from the west bank, which, upstream of the railway bridge, is high enough never to flood. The Avon was thrashing along. Where the main flow passed over salmon stones or depressions in the gravel there were quite violent upsurgings and downswirls. Though quick-flowing, the river normally runs silently; on that January day it sounded like the Colorado rapids. Yet the more powerfully the main river surged the more eagerly the fish would pack into the few quieter slacks and backwaters. The slack under the trees by the House Pool looked as if it should be bristling with barbel.

Naturally, the fishery was deserted and when I got to the chosen swim my rational self was still making pathetic attempts to talk me out of my enjoyment.

'You never waterproofed your Barbour,' it said. 'You'll get horribly, *horribly* wet. And nothing will bite in these conditions, except the cold. No one but you would be stupid enough to go fishing today. That's what Graham was saying. That's why no one else is here.'

I was standing, hunched up under the dripping trees, staring at the water. Then I noticed that only the trees were dripping. It had stopped raining. What is more, there was a beautiful blue hole in the grey above me.

'Told you so!' said my faithful self, who had persuaded me earlier on that the weather would break, despite the pessimism of the Met. Office. Just to placate my rational self I put my brolly up. If nothing else, it would be a shield against the rising wind.

I tackled up, using a 12-foot Fred J. Taylor roach rod, a centrepin loaded with 6-pound line, a small baiting engine (swimfeeder) and a size 10 hook. As I baited up with seven grubs my faithful self whispered, 'You're going to get one first cast.' Rational self said, 'If you hooked a barbel first cast you'd be so astonished you'd probably lose it.' I cast and, after only a minute, there was a trembling and flickering on the rod tip that I converted into a lovely hooping bend.

'Told you so,' said dominant self (it's his favourite phrase). It was going to be a good day.

I had not used the twelve-footer before on the Avon, but I was immediately conscious of its superb barbel-restraining qualities. It had such a precise, sensitive power range. When the fish hung in the quieter water I could just tease it over with the tip, but when it strove for the main flow I could apply the steely strength of the middle section and the fish would soon be circling back. Admittedly, it was not a big barbel, but a four-pounder in a strong current is a good test for any rod – especially a roach rod.

The clouds passed over, the sun shone. It was only 11 a.m. I was sure I would get a brace and became almost impatient after half an hour without another bite. I changed from seven to two maggots on the hook, then three. I had a nip-nip-nip sort of bite, which I missed. I tried four and cast again. After a few minutes there was another quick nip-nip, then nab-nab, which was positive enough, though when I struck I at first thought I must be solid in the rotting weedbeds. The rod's curve remained fixed, then it swayed a little and finally bucked into life.

As soon as the line began to inch off the reel I knew this was a much bigger

fish. It felt immensely strong, heaving the rod round into a leftward, upstream curve and making the tip stab and stab again. It dug deeply under the old weed-beds, almost sealing itself in, but each time the pulse of the tail stroke began to lock in the fronds I applied a little more side strain and the fish responded by ploughing even farther into sanctuary. At least I kept him on the move and though the weed stems were tough when bunched together they were also brittle.

It seemed an age before I finally had the contest going my way. I waded down to the right of the gap in the trees, gave the rod and line as much as they would bear and the barbel began to come back, then down, down, then round and up with a great swirl on the surface and he was hovering, in sight, just a rod-length away. I eased him towards me and offered thanks to the river god as a great amber flank was parcelled in the mesh.

A tremendous, portly, thick-backed fish of 8 pounds 9 ounces. Yet, as I was joyously feeding his golden image to my camera, a sudden tremendous gust of wind hit my brolly. Its anchor was uprooted and it took off, but not before

Another nine pounder from the Royalty.

scooping up every single item on the bank and tipping the whole lot in the swollen river. Creel, lunch box, rod, holdall (with rods), tackle tin, flashgun, camera bag (without camera), flash and float case – it all went in. And as I dived down the bank to grab what I could, my cap blew off and landed in midstream.

'Should've listened to me,' said rational self.

Amazingly, I recovered everything except my cap. I spotted a minute green dot, up a tree, a quarter of a mile away over the flooded fields and had to go wading and climbing to reach it. It took about an hour to sort myself out and drain the water from my holdall, bags and sandwiches. The flashgun still worked, though it gave out smoke as well as light.

I prepared to fish again and cast into the same part of the slack as before, a few yards short of the distinct crease between fast and slow water. The feeder settled and I waited, with the rod held out pointing downstream, feeling for the slightest change in pressure. After only two or three minutes the tip trembled and gave a tiny nod, exactly like the bite of a baby dace. I tapped the rod and was almost shocked to find myself once more locked into a barbel.

Again the heavy hanging, dour resistance, as if I'd been fused to the river; then the punching thrust of the tail, piling the pressure towards the breaking strain and sending the music of the reel up through the octaves.

A pike fisherman came wandering up the bank, the first person I'd seen on the bank all day. He said he liked the way the cane was bending and offered his services as a gillie. I stuttered a few words of reply and the barbel moved right and made a deep, slow, confident run downstream. It turned abruptly and planed out and away against the current, the line humming and whining in the wind.

The sun was shining brightly and I glimpsed a flash of bronze deep down in the blue water. I brought the fish steadily in for a few yards, then had to let the line pour off the drum again. It was obviously another good fish, but as it suddenly increased the power of its dive I realized that it might be something extra-special. When it eventually returned it rolled, just twelve feet out, making the water bulge and heave. My netsman made a professional job of the final moment and then a great, glistening barbel was lying in the wet grass, scalding my eyes.

'Might be a ten-pounder,' said my gillie. The balance hovered on 9 pounds 11 ounces.

I should have gone home then. The sky was still clear, but the horizon looked threatening. The wind was rising again and the temperature falling quickly. I presumed, though, that the fading light would make the already frisky barbel positively suicidal, so I fished on through the chilly, darkening afternoon and didn't even consider an early tea. I roundly cursed the gusting wind. Time and again the rod tip, held high, jiggered tantalizingly, only to be blown almost flat by a ferocious blast just as I was about to strike. Of course I did strike, but the timing wasn't right and I missed every bite except one. Another barbel. It burrowed deeply under the dead weed and took over five minutes – a real see-saw tug of war – before the clutching fronds gave way. Once in the open, the fish felt colossal, easily the biggest barbel I had hooked. When it finally turned and swept downstream I had no control. I knew it would certainly be lost if it got out of the slack and into the riotous main current, so I just clamped down at the last moment and prayed. It worked; the fish slowed and rose up to the surface, thrashing wildly with its tail. My gillie ran down the line of alders to see if he could get a clear view of it, but he shouted back to say that it wasn't a monster at all, just an average-sized barbel hooked in the pelvic.

It's amazing how much more firmly you can hold a fish when you suddenly realize it isn't the monster you had imagined. Yet though the 6-pound line was stretched to its absolute limit I could not get the fish back upstream, not with its flank broadside to the flow. However, without moving from my spot – which would have been difficult – I swung the barbel in under the bank twenty yards downstream, where the gillie netted it. It was about six pounds.

The heavy clouds released their load – first rain, then hail, then sleet and finally snow. The temperature continued to plummet and there was no more barbelish activity. On my last visit, with Ferret, the fish had begun to roll and porpoise in the evening light, but this time I saw nothing. Barbel are not fond of old-fashioned winter weather.

I had driven to the river through floods; now I drove home again along roads white with snow.

After our success in the winter, Ferret and I were eager to discover how the Royalty would fish in summer. We had fished it regularly from January to the

'Might be a ten pounder !' said my gillie.

season's end and, with one exception, had taken barbel on each visit, including two more nine-pounders and a dozen over eight pounds. Apart from the odd salmon, the only other fish we caught was a solitary chub, which, at 5 pounds 12 ounces, was my best ever.

We went again in July the following season and were much heartened by what we found. Of course it looked a changed world after our last visit, on a bleak March day. The river then was iron grey and the banks bare and mud-slicked; now it was shining in the morning sun, smooth along the deeps, broken and sparkling where it ran across the weed-rich shallows and all as transparent as glass. The banks were grown up with willow-herb, rush and buttercup; the lines of willows and alders provided a green curtain across the less desirable realities to the west. And the most gratifying element of all was the lack of human presence. It was a glorious summer day; no wind, cloudless sky, the air fresh and sweet. The river was in perfect order, yet, upstream of the railway bridge, there was only one other angler and he was prawning for salmon (with an Avocet, I was pleased to see).

'There are over three million anglers in this little country,' said Ferret, 'and I thought they'd all be here today.'

We walked up and down both banks, scanning the depths with polarizing glasses, and after about half an hour I found just the sort of swim I'd been looking for – a longish, narrow, clear run between dense beds of water buttercup and, up near its head, pale shadows that were barbel holding steady in the current. There were also darker, more active shapes moving amongst the barbel and these I guessed were chub and bream, though the run was almost in midstream and it wasn't possible to see clearly into it.

Ferret chose a pool beneath the pipe bridge where he'd spotted a group of fish, but he was so intrigued by my swim that he wanted to watch my first cast. I waded out over a firm gravel bed until I was about ten yards from the top of the run. At the given word, Ferret catapulted a pouchful of grubs and I couldn't help smiling as I saw the dark shapes of the midwater fish rise up towards the surface and the pale shadows of the barbel break ranks and turn quickly to left and right.

My rod was the twelve-footer again, with a $3^1/_2$-inch Aerial Popular and

136

6-pound line. I was going to use a squat, red-tipped fluted float and trot the maggots, on a size 12, down the length of the run. First cast, the float ran half-way along the swim before the line caught in a tuft of reeds. I flicked it back, cast again and it zipped under immediately. The fish I hooked felt lively and the line thrummed in the fast current.

'Chub!' I said, and Ferret agreed, especially when it flashed a white belly and pink fins. But it was tussling a little too tenaciously for a chub and I couldn't understand it. I gave the tackle all it could stand and the chub responded by streaking off downstream. The water broke, I told myself that the chub wasn't going any farther and it sent the spray flying. The rod shook wonderfully throughout its length. But then the chub made another, abrupt dive that I wasn't prepared for and the line snapped, cracking like a whip.

'Blimey!' said Ferret.

'Some chub,' I said, cursing my incompetence. Luckily the float came back and I had my hooks and shot in my pocket. Soon the red tip was sailing down-stream again and it wasn't long – about three casts later – before it swept under and the rod tip followed its direction. Another chub? It fought gamely and spiritedly, but I was more careful and this time I got it, persuading it up over the edge of the packed weedbed and sliding it bodily across the raft of stems. It wasn't a chub at all but a very bright – almost white-gold – barbel of $3\frac{1}{2}$ pounds. Of course that first fish, double the curse, had also been a barbel!

Still, to get the first barbel of the season on such a lovely summer morning, and on float tackle, was something to be jubilant about. And I was confident there would be more to follow.

Minutes later a miscast put the float on top of the weed raft at the head of the run. I twitched if off, it sank instantly and the rod hauled over before I realized what had happened. Ferret, sitting on the bank behind me, laughed and shouted something derogatory. However, after a couple of minutes the hook pulled free. He catapulted in some more maggots and immediately I saw again the deep, curving forms of barbel, like a cluster of sabres, materializing from beneath the streamer weed. Down went the float – again a lovely, decisive dive, slanting back upstream as it disappeared. The rod bent into a satisfying resist-ance which held firm yet dynamically in the current. Then the explosive rush downstream and across, making the reel sing.

Within an hour I'd landed four but lost five, yet only that first fish had broken me. Then I started timing the strike better, or else the barbel just began feeding more earnestly, for I lost no more and netted another four fish, the best going 5$\frac{1}{2}$ pounds. After that one I took a break and waded ashore for a cup of tea and a rest.

'There must be a hundred barbel in that swim,' I said to Ferret, who had not had a bite in his chosen pool. 'Come down and have a cast. You'll definitely get one.'

He waded out and I sat back in the sun, on the grass, eating my sandwiches, watching him fishing. I had given him my rod to use and he soon got the rhythm of it. After ten minutes he hooked a fish which didn't pull very hard; in fact it was straight away flapping ineffectively on the surface. Much to Ferret's dismay it was a three-pound bream. Without too much effort he caught four more.

'Look here!' I said. 'Stop mucking about. Every time I 'pult in a pouchful of maggots I can *see* the barbel. The swim is paved with them.'

Ferret cast again and hooked a bootlace eel.

'It's no good,' I said, 'I'll just have to demonstrate, so you'll see what you're doing wrong.'

Big-head tackled up the Wallis Wizard and dropped a swim feeder into the ribbon-width fissure in the weeds above the main run. After a minute there was a quick tug, followed by a firmer pull and straight away I knew it wasn't a bream.

'I don't believe it!' said Ferret.

I worked the fish gradually downstream, almost under Ferret's nose, and eventually a five-pound barbel rolled into the net. Inspired by my example, Ferret caught a baby chub.

'We're running out of bait,' I said. 'I'll guarantee you a fish by going to get another couple of pints. Without my unendurable presence you're bound to succeed.'

I only got as far as the Railway pool. I'd just paused there to chat to the salmon angler with the Avocet when there came a triumphant shout from upstream. He'd got one at last and even managed to land it with me standing behind him making unhelpful comments. It was the best of the day, just over

138

The rod hauled over before I realised what had happened.

seven pounds (the rascal).

By the time I returned with replenishments and refreshments (two cartons of fruit juice, because it was hot work) Ferret had caught another. I allowed him to land one more and lose a good fish of perhaps the same size as the first. Unfortunately it rolled off at the net, a heart-rending sight. Then I returned to the fray, while he took the lazy angler's option and lounged on the bank with the feeder rod.

I suffered with the inconsistency for which I'm famous and completely lost my rhythm. To fish the run effectively the float had to fall perfectly, with the shot and hookbait landing in a direct line beyond it, about three or four inches from the surface weed at the run's head. All the fish had been taken in the first ten feet of the swim down, where the water was deepest. Once into the shallower stretch the tackle was whipped out and immediately flicked back to the starting point. But if the rhythm was too pronounced and vigorous the bait ended up on the surface weed and probably got stuck there. If the cast was too timid the tackle fell short and the bait would not settle properly in the hot spot.

It was four o'clock on a fine, now breezy afternoon. We had ample supplies of bait and surely I could not keep the rod straight during the entire five hours before the sun set. Gradually, I got the flow back into my fishing, the float bobbed and I hooked a barbel which pulled heavily and kept tight to the riverbed, nosing upstream under the weed. It delved into the densest part of the bed, the worst part, on my side of the run, and plugged itself deep into the enveloping fronds. I couldn't shift it, nor could I reach it, at least not with thigh waders, so I went ashore, removed waders and trousers and, under a barrage of catcalls from Ferret, strove courageously out into the eel-infested river. But, though I managed to reach the fish in about four foot of water, I could not clear the tangle of weed fingers that enfolded it. It didn't like the look of my knees either and bolted suddenly, straightening the fine wire hook.

Next I caught a bored-looking bream, then two more barbel, a four and a six-pounder. The bream, also around four pounds, took about fifteen seconds to land, the two barbel about five minutes each. The difference between a barbel and a bream is the difference between a rocket and a drowned slug.

I gave the rod back to Ferret and downed a carton of fruit juice while he put on a barbel fisher's exhibition performance, landing two and losing one all inside ten minutes. Then nothing for half an hour and I called him ashore.

'Come in number six, or I'll drink all your pineapple juice!'

We finished off our food and took stock of the bait situation. Not good. We had used almost three-quarters of a gallon of maggots and had about half an hour's supply remaining. But we did have alternatives and I opened a can of sweetcorn and waded out again. The bait was in a bag over my shoulder and I tossed in a handful every other cast. It was interesting how I could cast consistently accurately *except* at that crucial moment that followed a free offering of groundbait. Finally I did it properly, the hookbait sinking down with the loose grains in precisely the right spot. The float travelled only a yard before it dipped under and I connected with a five-pounder. The next cast was again exactly right and I intuitively knew that I was going to get the best of the day. I almost said, 'This is it!' but wisely remained silent. Had I spoken, nothing would have happened. Down went the float and away went a deeply surging barbel.

'This one feels a bit better,' I said.

Luckily he kept well out on the opposite side of the swim and, because I kept the pressure to the absolute maximum, he stubbornly refused to cross over to my side. This was just how I wanted it. After some heavy barging into the weeds upstream, he swept down and smashed the surface, then wheeled up and under a raft of streamers and scythed through them with his tail. He surfaced and I saw that he wasn't enormous, or even very big, but, as I'd predicted, he was the biggest of my day. Eventually I slid him over the net. Not only the biggest, but also the best. Richly coloured, his vitality almost exploded out of his golden shell. He was six and three-quarter pounds.

Meanwhile, Ferret had another brace on the Wizard using legered corn. I carried on with the float and found myself surrounded by bream. I must have had six, all around four pounds, before I said, 'The next one comes home for the badgers!'

After that I never had another bite. Both bream and barbel simply vanished. Ferret persevered with the leger as the sun sank beyond the willows on the far bank, but he also had no more chances.

The evening gently descended. One or two bats skimmed across the surface and a pale mist began to dull the river's gleam.

CHAPTER SEVENTEEN

Barbus Maximus

~

I have always been fascinated by the way Nature seems to relax her own rules when she dives underwater. Though the majority of fishes are all clad in their proper uniforms there will always be a few nonconformists flashing unconventional colour schemes or showing off weird variations of tone, shade or even form. But while there are rare examples of such eccentricity in the mammal and bird kingdoms you will never find, say, a seventy-pound badger or a penguin ten feet tall. The record books, however, are full of fish twice as big as they should be. Nature seems to revel in such extremes, as if she enjoys the surprise it gives us. She teases the freshwater biologist and makes him worry about his standards.

Imagine a horse fourteen feet high or an elephant twice as big as a house. These things are not possible on land, but, in the buoyant, weightless world below the surface, anything is possible. A British carp of twenty-five pounds is much larger than the average size for the species, yet we know they can grow twice as big and I've seen one three times larger.

In a world ruled and chastened by statistics and conforming routine it's refreshing that there should still be room for such anomalies. They are somehow reassuring. My interest in giant fish stems from an angler's instinctive yearning for a big catch, but even if I wasn't an angler I'd still be fascinated by gigantism. Everyone is fascinated by monsters, and if they are beautiful monsters so much the better. I have no real ambition to catch a record-size barbel, just as I had no ambition to catch a record carp, but I like the idea of such a fish and I always enjoy reading and listening to stories about them.

What is or was the biggest barbel in Britain? Contemporary sceptics pour scorn over the old tales of fish approaching twenty pounds, yet I and others have seen a barbel in the mid-teens of pounds and if a fish can reach that size today, what was the growth potential when there was no pollution, weed cutting or abstraction?

There is a wonderful account in B B's *Fisherman's Bedside Book* written by an old Thames professional, J. L. Webb, of a dramatic battle with a barbel that Webb swore weighed twenty pounds. It broke him in the end yet, at one stage during the fight, he'd had it over his net. J. W. Martin, writing a hundred years ago, told of a Trent barbel caught on a nightline that weighed over eighteen pounds and there was a story of a fish only a pound less from the Kennet in the early 1900s. In 1924 Roy Beddington had a 16¼-pounder from the Royalty, fairly hooked on a spun dace. The fish was weighed by the head keeper, M. W. Hayter, who was said to be a stickler for accuracy. He himself foul-hooked a barbel of 15¾ pounds and had observed other, much larger fish. I have seen the mounted 14 pound 6 ounce specimen caught by Aylmer Tryon in 1934. That also came from the Royalty. It is a huge-looking fish, more impressive than the other famous cased barbel of sixteen pounds, which was foul-hooked at Ibsley Weir in 1961. (There were two other fish of 14 pounds 6 ounces, one caught in 1888, from the Thames, and the other from the Royalty in 1937 taken by the barbel expert F. W. K. Wallis. There were also four other reputed fourteen-pounders – all from the Royalty).

But, like Webb's monster, the biggest barbel were never landed. Most of them were never even seen. There was a colossal corpse of a fish long dead, found floating on the Great Weir of the Royalty. It was dragged out and several reputable anglers claim it must have weighed nearly twenty pounds in its prime.

Richard Walker once had an addiction a bit like mine for barbel fishing. With Pete Thomas and Fred J. Taylor he spent many days pursuing a colony of large fish which patrolled the Avon below Ibsley Weir. Early in the season most of these barbel would be together in small shoals. Writing in Peter Wheat's *The Fighting Barbel*, Richard says he once (1 July 1964) saw a shoal of a dozen fish and half of them were over the record, which was then, as it is now, held by Tryon's fourteen-pounder. Writing to me, he said there were barbel at Ibsley in the 1960s which were undoubtedly as big as twenty pounds and maybe bigger. He,

Pete and Fred had seen them, and also Colonel Crow, the river keeper, who had a good eye for a twenty-pound salmon. Yet in eight years he caught just three fish at Ibsley and, though the largest of them was the biggest barbel he ever caught, it was still, at $12^3/_4$ pounds, a dwarf compared with the monsters.

Thirteen-pounders are still occasionally taken from the vicinity of Ibsley bridge, but, almost certainly, there are no more barbel as large as those seen thirty years ago. Farther upstream, towards Salisbury, who knows?

By a strange coincidence, my own biggest Ibsley fish came from a pool only a few yards upstream of where Richard caught his best barbel. And, as is the way with these quirks of fate, my fish also weighed $12^3/_4$ pounds. But there the similarity ends, as I shall recount.

It was a fine September day and I'd gone down to Ibsley with Colonel Ray Kemp, proposing to catch a barbel or two on the float. The Colonel fished up towards the Harbridge Stream, I fished the Hut Pool, wading out across the gravel shallows above and trotting my float along the deep gulley under the far bank. Third cast – I was using double maggot on a size 12 hook and 5-pound line – the float vanished about a quarter of the way along the pool. The strike set the Avocet into a severe, barely quivering bend. A fish kicked once, then moved extremely slowly and very determinedly downstream.

'With barbel,' R. W. wrote to me, 'you can never tell, for the first few seconds, whether it's a three- or a thirteen-pounder. They all feel like monsters when you strike them.'

This one persisted in feeling like a monster. It reached the tail of the pool, where the long tresses of water buttercup fingered the surface, and I thought it would continue through the shallows and down to the next pool. I eased off a fraction and the fish immediately stopped, circled round the upper edge of the weedbeds and came slowly and ominously towards me. All the time its movements were deliberate and almost at snail's pace. It kept low to the riverbed. It was obviously a very big barbel.

I shouted and whistled and eventually the Colonel came hurrying downstream and threw the net out to me. I was trying not to move too much, I didn't want to cause the monster to panic off downstream. Though I only had light tackle, I felt that I might be able to at least tease it close enough to be able to

You can never tell, for the first few seconds, whether it's
a three or a thirteen pounder.

A splendid, bright, fresh run; sublimely disappointing fish.

glimpse it. The Colonel offered encouraging words and said it was obviously the barbel of a lifetime. It took off again down the pool, but the release of pressure again did the trick and, like a conductor during the quietest passage of a concerto, I leant tensely forward and just stroked the air with the rod, keeping the temperature down and yet all the time cozening and cajoling, edging the virtuoso soloist towards the triumphant finale – in my landing net. Suddenly there was a new sensation, a sort of thrumming on the line, and then a great fish rocketed vertically up through the surface to be greeted by a hail of abuse from me and a howl of laughter from the Colonel.

'It's a —— silver tourist'! I wailed. I've hooked and landed quite a few salmon while barbel fishing, up to $17^{1}/_{2}$ pounds, but, with one exception, I knew from the strike, as one does, that it was a tourist. This was not a salmon, however, but a big sea trout and, as I said, it weighed over twelve pounds. A splendid, bright, fresh-run, sublimely disappointing fish – but for a while it was my biggest barbel.

The same kind of thing happened on the Wye between Hay and Hereford. The stretch was leased by Terry Wright, who was then landlord of the Kingfisher Inn at Hay. He'd seen some very big barbel as well as some enormous chub. He led the way to a deep pool where, a few hours before, he'd had an extravagant catch of chub and dace and where he was convinced a barbel was lying.

Just after sunset, as I was rolling a sliver of spam through the centre of the pool, I had a half-hearted take which became a full-blooded downstream rush as soon as I struck. The pool was fairly clear of weed and other obstructions but my 4-pound line was soon stretching through two weedbeds, the nearest one thirty yards below us. I immediately guessed it was a salmon, but Terry said he wasn't sure. It had gone straight for the weed, which salmon, being one of nature's dimwits, rarely think to do. When I'd worked it back and it began circling, remaining deep and sullen, Terry was convinced that it really couldn't be a silver tourist and I was becoming convinced, too, though I was still suspicious.

It was dark by the time it surfaced and I was still not sure. If it was a chub it was going to be unbelievable; if it was a barbel it was going to be big, but if it was a $10^{1}/_{4}$-pound hen salmon I'd bite chunks out of my rod butt and chase Terry along the bank with a gaff.

The Wye is a magnificent river. I visit it every year and have spent many happy days fishing for its chub, dace and elusive barbel, and occasionally casting a deliberate line for salmon. However I regard the Avon, I know a time may come when the Wye's compelling nature might get the better of me. Before we moved to Cranborne Chase the Gaffer and I came very close to buying a cottage at Hay. The angling potential is unlimited and though there are not great numbers of barbel they are increasing their range and growing bigger all the time. It's a difficult water to fish, being moody, unpredictable and inscrutable, but, unlike the Avon, the Wye is a truly wild, untramelled river: there are no dredgers; there are not even any artificial weirs. And the landscape is often spectacularly beautiful. Also, Redmire is nearby. If I had two hundred years to live I would fish the Avon until I was a hundred, then spend my last century on the Wye – for that is how long it would take to get to know the river properly. I have no doubt that a record-size barbel is swimming in the reddish-tinted water even as I write.

The biggest barbel I ever saw was in the Parlour pool on the Royalty, in July 1985. I was with the Colonel again, leaning over the parapet of the bridge that spans the pool. Several barbel were milling about below us but we had not seen anything that looked much over eight or nine pounds. One of the workmen from the pumping station came up next to us, smiled slightly sheepishly, said good morning, and tossed in a whole can of sweetcorn. We watched the cascade of yellow grains sinking into the turbulent water and then the Colonel and I started shouting. An immense barbel rose up from the darkness below us and curved through the drifting corn, engulfing it like a whale filtering plankton. It was three feet long and its back looked as broad as a spaniel's.

'Yup,' said the workman, 'she's a lunker all right!'

As the grains slowly sank, the fish was gradually lost from view.

'How big was that?' I said.

'Twice as big as anything else down there,' said the Colonel.

'She must be sixteen pound,' said the workman, turning and walking back towards the pumping station. It seemed quite a conservative estimate. I rushed round to my creel, along the bank, grabbed the bait box and within seconds another cloud of corn was descending into the depths. The monster returned immediately and this time it was accompanied by four others, all good fish, one of them perhaps twelve pounds. Yet they seemed almost shrunken and puny next to the great matriarch. She shouldered her way through the pack and the wash created by her huge pectorals must have been enough to fling even the twelve-pounder sideways. It wasn't quite as extraordinary as seeing the king of Redmire, but it was still an astounding sight.

We looked downstream towards the oppressive noticeboard hanging from the chain which stretched the width of the pool. 'No Fishing Above the Chain', it read, a warning to those evil persons who sought to hang over the parapet and foul-hook salmon for the pot. But we were not evil persons. Nor did we wish for a salmon, though we had paid £50 for our day's fishing and were legally entitled to any we caught.

Ken Keynes, the head bailiff, came up, materializing as bailiffs are wont to do whenever anglers lean towards temptation. 'No,' he said, quite firmly, yet not unkindly, we had better not fish above the chain. So we fished on the bank below, just ten yards from the monster's lair. I caught eight barbel to eight pounds and we released some of them under the parapet, to see if our estimates of size seemed accurate. The eight-pounder looked about as big as a record gudgeon. The Colonel caught a carp and lost three fish, one of which smashed him almost casually, taking a leisurely turn round a bit of stonework and effectively sawing the line in two.

The Colonel's friend, Mike Skitrall, had a Parlour day the next week. He was carefully briefed and ordered not to use anything other than a carp or salmon rod and 12-pound line. Cunningly, Mike also used a float with a long tail and allowed the back-flow to drift his bait towards the desired spot while his float remained stationary, outside the total exclusion zone. His companion tossed in free offerings and shouted instructions when the monster finally appeared. Mike's star was in the ascendant – for a while. He somehow avoided the lesser fish and eventually managed to hook the big one.

'I had it under control for most of the time,' Mike told me later. 'It just went round and round under the chain and didn't even make a bid for the downstream weedbeds.'

After a few minutes a gallery had collected on the bridge and they all gasped and then groaned as Mike's hook pulled free.

Later on, using the same technique, Mike's pal hooked the second biggest barbel, which we'd thought was twelve pounds. It was eleven and three-quarters.

She was still occupying the pool when we returned a year later. Several anglers had cast baits at her but she'd eluded them all. The Colonel and I planned to use Mike's simple but effective trick and we spun a coin to decide who had first cast. I won.

The Colonel tossed in the attractor and, amazingly, the first fish to show was the giantess. She came boldly and massively down beneath the chain, clearly visible to the Colonel, and she snaffled every bit of Bacon Grill she could see, including the bit on my hook. I knew I probably wouldn't see the float move. It was unshotted and there was a long tail, at least ten feet. So I relied on the Colonel to shout orders from his high vantage-point and I was watching him as his face showed signs of boggled astonishment. He gave me a double thumbs-up, but I hesitated because we had agreed that I would do nothing until he gave the word. Unfortunately that word was jammed somewhere along his throat and when he finally croaked 'Strike!' it was too late. I had embedded a size 6 Mustad in a huge chunk of Grill and yet when I struck the bait had gone from the hook. The Colonel said he had clearly seen the monster grab it, but the tension was too much and he was rendered speechless at the crucial moment. We caught plenty of other barbel that day but we never saw the big one again.

The biggest barbel I have seen on the bank was of quite modest dimensions compared with that Parlour fish and my own biggest seems a positive tiddler. The former was a twelve-pounder caught by Ferret in September 1984.

Ferret took it just after moonrise at the end of a fifteen-hour day which produced just two other fish. However, the day would have been memorable even without the barbel. We had begun fishing at first light, on a lovely overgrown stretch of the Avon below Ringwood. Ferret fished his favourite swim, which we called Upstairs, and I fished Slumber Pool, at the lower end of the fishery. We were joined at sunrise by a number of other barbel fanatics, but no one had even a bite until mid-morning, when Ferret landed a fish of 9 pounds 6 ounces.

At noon someone else caught an eel and a chub. A large hawk came winging

Ferret with his example of Barbus Maximus.

down river, driving a dozen cormorants out of a nearby tree. It was an osprey, the first one I had ever seen in the valley. It took up a position at the top of the tree and defended it all afternoon against crows, rooks, cormorants and a kestrel. Two or three times it swooped across the water, eventually diving on a fish and catching it. I think it was a small pike. Towards evening it glided off down river, continuing its journey south for the winter.

The sun set, the moon rose and a dense mist began to form. At last light I had my first bite and this was a barbel of 9½ pounds. Invariably Ferret catches the best of the day, but this time I'd just pipped him. As I felt my way upstream through the mist to blow a raspberry at him, he came blundering down to blow one at me. We hurried to his swim and there in his net was the big barbel. It glistened in the moonlight and looked, as Ferret said, 'as big as a horse'. He'd taken it on a tiny square of luncheon meat dropped just over the bankside reeds. Together our three fish weighed a fraction under thirty-one pounds and they were the only barbel from the fishery that day.

My own largest barbel was a bit of a joke, a bit of a dream and a bit of unforgivable conceit. Sandy 'Adipose' Leventon was, in 1984, features editor for *Angling Times* and, bored with the interminable 'Boom Time Burbot Bonanza on the Borkshire Baine!' type of article, he decided to inject some style into his paper.

'I think the Golden Scale Club should have a barbel expedition to the Royalty,' he told me.

'You mean,' I said, '"Bewildered Barbel Belaboured by Blaspheming Bygones"?'

'No!' he replied. 'I'm going to call the article "Cane and Able" and you're going to write it!'

'If you treat us to supper afterwards, we'll do it.'

'What do you think you'll catch?' asked Adipose.

'I'll get you an eleven-pounder!'

And so it was, on a bitter November day, that seven members of the G. S. C. were press-ganged into a piscatorial display. There was Parker, Henry, Ferret, the Colonel, Harry, Berol and I and we fished with a vengeance, eager to show the world that split cane and centrepin reels were all you required to ensure a basket of bountiful barbel. We all blanked. No, that's not true. Ferret got a six-pounder and Harry caught a barrowful, including an eight-pounder. But Adipose and his photographer, Bill, were severely crestfallen.

'You promised me an eleven-pounder!' whined Adipose. 'I believed you, and so did Bill.'

'"Bill Bemoans Barbel Blankers"?' said Parker, miserably. 'At least it would be an honest account.'

'If you'd all blanked,' said Adipose, 'we could have made a story out of it, but this was neither one thing nor the other.' It didn't help matters to have supper at a famous fishing pub at Downton which had recently had its atmosphere renovated.

The day had begun with Henry's car breaking down and we thought that a bad omen at the time. I now realized that it gave us the opportunity for a second chance.

*Members of the Golden Scale Club assemble on the
Royalty fishery (from top left, clockwise, Harry, Berol,
Colonel, Henry, Ferret, Ferneyhough, Parker).*

'Henry's car won't be fixed till tomorrow evening,' I said. 'So he and I will
have another day on the Royalty and this time I *will* get you an eleven pounder.'

I made this infantile boast before eight witnesses and they all yawned and
turned back to their drinks.

The next day was like spring after winter. The breeze was soft, the sun warm,
but not too bright, the river full of eternal promise. Henry and I went up to the
Great Weir and we put a pint of maggots into the slack by the weir tail, where
Harry had caught his barbel the day before. Henry had a bite first cast and minutes later I hooked a good fish. Henry took the photographs as I eventually slid

154

Henry said something ungodly. I said 'Eleven pounds !'

an eight-pound barbel over the net. Then Henry hooked a fish and I picked up the camera. Adipose would be pleased. What with the previous day's episode, there was enough material for an article and we hadn't even had lunch yet.

First cast of the afternoon I hooked a fish (on a size 6 and about a dozen maggots) which just mooched off nonchalantly towards the centre of the weir-pool. Increasing or decreasing pressure had no effect and it took twenty yards off a reel which didn't sing but just said 'click-click-click-click-click'. Finally the fish slowed and rose up a little in the water and the main force of the weir and the strain of the line turned it and brought it grudgingly back. It surfaced close in, with a sweeping flash of gold, and then launched itself straight down the weir tail. I could have pursued it, but didn't. I slowed and stopped it, then patiently brought it back against the flow and led it upstream of the net before allowing it to turn down again – straight into the mesh.

It looked like a good nine-pounder, but when I lifted the net out of the water I got a pleasant surprise and said to Henry, 'This is bigger than I thought.' Of course we didn't like to say what it might weigh. Simply to mention the subject was enough to make the fish vanish before our eyes. For once it seemed as if the statistics mattered. I zeroed the scales and, with apologies, put the glorious barbel tenderly into the weigh sling. We gawped as the pointer came to rest precisely on the required mark. Not a dram more or less.

Henry said something ungodly. I said, 'Eleven pounds!' and we both burst out laughing.

CHAPTER EIGHTEEN

Redmire: The Film

I n all the countless journeys I'd made to Redmire I'd never felt anything other than a happy anticipation at the prospect of returning to my favourite carp pool. However, in June 1989, eight years after my previous visit, my pleasure was mixed with a certain amount of apprehension. I was going to Redmire with the internationally famous wildlife film maker Hugh Miles, and for the first time in my life it was essential that I caught a big carp. Hugh was going to make a fishing film and there was a twenty-pounder in the script.

Hugh had booked the pool at great expense for the first ten days of the season and, although my own experiences of that period had all been good, there had been numerous opening weeks which had been very poor – in fact the previous season opened with a complete blank. To make matters worse, the angling press had got wind of the project and phoned me for a few details. I rashly stated that I was confident of success and had never before blanked at Redmire during opening week. I immediately regretted my words. Fate takes great pleasure in deflating people who tempt her like that and, as I said earlier, there was a little demon at Redmire who could tie an angler's line into knots, and the angler as well if he started taking things for granted.

Had Hugh been relying solely on me I think I might have been really worried, but there was a third in the party, Bob 'Breeks' James, a superbly consistent piscator who could be relied upon to provide the poundage, even though he used carbon rods and other such examples of technological trumpery.

We converged on the pool two days before the season began, hoping to prepare filming and fishing stations so that everything would be ready for the cameras to roll on opening morning.

After my long history of carp addiction had been cured by barbel fishing I had no intention of going back to Redmire, at least not to fish. And the idea of making films about fishing had always seemed questionable to me, even slightly lunatic. Several such approaches had been made to me in the past and I had, after consideration, turned them all down.

The camera is myopic, it can only record a limited part of the scene; yet, to be convincing, a fishing film must not only reveal the watery scene in as much detail as possible, it must also convey the atmosphere, excitement, sounds and poetry of angling, harmonizing all these elements naturally. Not an easy task.

(Of course, here I scrawl, attempting this same task with a pen. Yet whatever limitations I have as a writer, I have the advantage over a film maker in that the pen is not constrained by technical considerations, ink is cheaper than film and, ultimately, the written word goes deeper, assimilated into the imagination, while a filmed object is predigested, more for the eyes alone.)

Hugh had secretly nursed this wild idea of making a fishing film for over twenty years. In the meantime he built up a reputation as probably the most talented, imaginative, committed and successful wildlife film maker in the world, with a string of international awards to his name. (He also happens to be a brilliant roach angler.)

In 1986 Hugh read my book *Casting at the Sun* and saw in it certain possibilities for film making. He phoned me and we talked about his ideas. Perhaps the thought of a fishing film did not seem so impossible after all. Here was a person who savoured the spirit of angling in nearly the same way as I did, but who also happened to be a great film maker. 'And, if we fail,' he said, 'it will still have been good fun to have tried'.

Hugh felt that the time was right to make a series of films about fishing which didn't dwell on piscatorial technique but instead concentrated on angling's essential magic. Days in the life of an angler would surely not be as difficult to film as the life of a polar bear, leopard, otter, condor or osprey, especially if the angler was regarded in the same light as these creatures, something not to be disturbed at any cost.

After our conversation I mulled over Hugh's proposal. He didn't want me to write the script; he wanted me to play the part. Was it feasible? Was it sane?

158

The carp were, as ever, impressive but Redmire was
magnificent.

Hugh's main concern was that such a project should not be allowed to disrupt our normal enjoyment of life and fishing; if it did, we would simply drop it. So really there was no dangerous commitment here. It might be interesting to attempt something so different and novel, and it would be a privilege to work with a genius. I'd do it. But it would probably be better, especially if we were producing a series, to have another angler involved, and who better than Bob? Despite his dubious attitudes to material things, Bob appreciates the true spirit of angling, is also a consummate all-rounder, can repair a broken reel with his eyes shut, casts a fly as well as he throws a frisbee and falls in with complete equanimity. He also has a dog which can retrieve hooked fish better than a professional gillie.

At midnight on 16 June, Hugh, Bob and I (but not Bob's dog) sat on the dam at Redmire, opened a bottle of champagne and fired off a signal rocket. We toasted the glory of Redmire, for we had all been impressed and enchanted by what we had seen; we toasted the new project, for the more we had discussed it the more enthusiastic we had become; we toasted the name of Isaak Walton and hoped he might smile on our endeavours. Then we cast, simultaneously, though this was purely a token gesture, part of the ritual, an hour's communal fishing while we drank the champagne and savoured the beginning of the new season. After the hour, Bob would creep off to his baited swim, near Pitchford's Pitch, under the poplars on the eastern bank, and I would just creep about, hoping to hear or sense signs of feeding fish in the dark. Hugh would get his head down for three hours and sleep till sunrise.

Since our arrival we had had ample opportunity to observe the carp and watch their reactions to all the various baits we offered. My confidence had grown considerably when I saw how eagerly they nosed down for such things as sprouted lentils, maggots and bramble jelly paste bombs. Even more encouraging was their response to the floating biscuits we scattered across them. Redmire carp had always been famous for their quirky refusal to take food from the top when surface feeding is second nature to any normal carp. Suddenly they had changed their habits, which meant I could adopt my favourite method of fishing. Maybe I would catch something after all.

The carp were, as ever, impressive, but Redmire was magnificent. I know the

pool – three acres of crystal-clear water in the rolling border country of Here-
fordshire – better than any other fishery, and yet, as I wrote earlier, my last visit
had not been auspicious and I felt our relationship had become jaded and stale.
Now, after a long separation, it was as if an old friend had welcomed me with
open arms, having forgiven some past, petty misunderstanding. And the pool
looked just as beautiful as ever, calm and serene in its lush midsummer raiment.
And the smell of it! As sweet as a bowl of fresh salad, as exotic as a jungle.

Redmire is a unique microcosm, a small planet orbited by birds, insects, rep-
tiles, carp anglers, amphibians and mammals; inhabited by an almost fantastic
number of big and resplendent carp. I have caught a fifty-pounder there, but I
have also seen five other fish which were unquestionably larger, including a
common carp too stupendous to be real. Yet it was real. Of course, nowadays,
most people believe the monsters are all dead and some believe they were never
more than myths. Fortunately, I wasn't the only person to behold the giants so
there is no good reason to disbelieve their historical existence. Whether any
exist now, no one can say with certainty. They were ever mysterious. Hugh,
Bob and I spent hours hoping to glimpse one of the old patriarchs, yet the biggest we saw was 'only' about thirty or thirty-five pounds. However, we were
privileged to witness the carp's annual spawning and Hugh got some splendid
footage of the fish as they careered and thrashed across the shallows, lifting
unfortunate coots and moorhens completely out of the water.

Hugh fell under Redmire's spell almost from the first moment he saw it and,
though we weren't fishing then, he spent most of his time filming. He focused
on every aspect and facet of the place. He was up before light on the first day (we
had a camp under the bankside oaks) so that he could film the dawn mist, then
the sun rising through it, and he was still filming when the sun went down again
sixteen hours later. He built a scaffold tower and two hides. He was up, as promised, at first light on the sixteenth and so was ready and waiting when I cast for
a carp in the shallow weedy corner of the dam, near the overspill. I had previously scattered some bait in this area and crept back at sunrise to see a large
fish, tail up, over the offerings. I cautiously waded into the margins, under the
trees opposite the overspill, and flicked another bait into the weedbeds. (Tackle
was the original Mark IV, which had last been to Redmire in September 1952, a

1934 Hardy Altex II loaded with 1989 8-pound Ultima, a braided trace and a size 8 Mustad.)

We had rather a long time to wait but I didn't mind because, now I was actually fishing, I felt myself merging back into Redmire's atmosphere, almost as if I were becoming transparent – invisible to the carp and closer to them, close enough to predict their movements. So when, finally, the bait was surreptitiously snaffled and the loose line drew taut I was not so self-conscious, hardly aware of Hugh's camera and less liable to break on the strike.

A big bow wave surged off parallel with the dam wall, heading for deeper water. The angle of the line cut into overhanging boughs on my right and I quickly waded out into open water. As the carp turned and began moving powerfully up the deep centre channel I shouted for Bob to bring the net. He'd been stalking fish way up at the pool's head and by the time he'd raced down, grabbed the net and joined me in the water, I had the fish circling close to the

162

It was a good one, it was fully scaled, the magic was still in the old cane.

surface, only ten yards away. Hugh, behind the camera on the dam, shouted directions; I ignored them, or rather, did not hear them, being deaf and blind to everything but the carp. It was a good one, it was fully scaled, the magic was still in the old cane, Bob was being a good gillie, the fish was coming, nearer, nearer.... and with a last flurry and swirl the net was rising and a 24-pound common carp was hammocked in the mesh.

We had radio microphones clipped onto our shirts and I'm sure I was talking gibberish as we waded ashore, filmed all the time by Hugh. He was pleased and delighted. Bob was pleased. I was just relieved. After we had photographed and ceremoniously released the fish I collapsed, smiling, under the willows.

At sunset I got an eleven-pounder, float-fishing in the shallows, but Bob had to wait until noon the next day before he had his first chance and his first ever Redmire carp. It was another 24-pounder, a leather, and the circumstances surrounding its capture were so bizarre that I have been sworn to secrecy until the film is eventually shown on television. All I shall say now is that the fishing was of the highest quality and Bob fell in again, taking me with him.

On the third day, stalking from one of Redmire's islands, I hooked another big fish and once more Hugh captured all the drama. After the initial power dive the carp lodged solid in weed and I was just wondering whether to go boating when it suddenly charged out into open water. I stayed in tenuous contact, but finally the vintage rod charmed another fully scaled fish into the net. It was one of the most perfect, classic-looking carp I have ever seen and it pulled the balance to a fraction over twenty-three pounds. We couldn't quite believe how it was all going precisely to plan. Even the weather was perfect. Every day the sun climbed into a clear sky and the dawn mist was quickly dispersed. There would be just enough breeze at midday to keep the fish moving on the shallows and even without the breeze we could always find carp basking in the weedbeds. The evenings were still and luminous and the carp fisher's moon was waxing.

I think, though, we must have started taking our good fortune for granted for on the fifth day we had a sudden string of minor catastrophes. Bob lost a very big fish in the weeds, about an hour before dawn. Then Hugh, who had become strangely enthusiastic about carp fishing and, at intervals between filming, would creep about with an ancient Mark IV Avon, also had some bad luck. At sunrise he was fishing for a group of carp under the oaks when his car door, which had been open, suddenly and inexplicably slammed shut. The carp fled and never returned. That morning Hugh had to deliver some exposed film to the local Red Star office, but, for the first time in his car's history, the battery was flat. Then Bob discovered he'd lost his car keys and Bob *never* loses his car keys. We eventually managed to get Hugh's Volvo going and while he was away I fished for gudgeon with his carbon rod. I hooked a carp, it dived into weed and the tip of the rod splintered and slanted down the line. Then the carp got off. Redmire's little demon was at work again, though when Hugh heard about his favourite roach rod he said the demon was not little at all; it was over six feet tall, wore a Norfolk jacket and a tweed cap and had no appreciation of carbon fibre. However, we did agree that we were perhaps beginning to snatch at Redmire's favours rather too greedily. We were becoming presumptuous. So we all sat on the dam and apologized profusely. Then, instead of fishing for carp, we spent the afternoon floating a frisbee across the fields.

In the evening we fished for gudgeon. Hugh decided we should also fish for gudgeon the next dawn, from the punt, in the manner of the traditional gudgeon scratcher. He would film our performance from the bank and the person who caught the most fish would win a bottle of champagne.

We pushed out of the boathouse a little after five o'clock. The moon was still quite clear in the west and the sun was just rising, sending beams quivering through the mist, tingeing it with gold. As we paddled across the glass-calm water we seemed to be engulfed in amber-coloured smoke. Far off, we heard a big fish turning on the surface but, when we looked towards the sound, we couldn't see even a glint of ripple. It was the perfect dawn for – gudgeon.

'This is probably illegal,' said Bob.

'Perhaps it should be,' I said. 'The Carp Society should decree that anyone found gudgeon fishing at Redmire will be banned for life.'

I had always reckoned that I was a bit of a specialist at gudgeon fishing, yet Bob won the match easily. But there were two glasses in the creel and so we shared a champagne breakfast, sitting in the punt, in the middle of Redmire, on midsummer morning.

As the mist cleared we could discern a pale figure standing in the shallows, up

As the mist cleared we could discern a pale figure
standing in the shallows.

Gudgeon fishing at dawn on Midsummer Day.

at the top of the pool. He was wearing a wide-brimmed straw hat and a full-length riding coat and he was fishing, or at least seemed to be. He was as still as a heron and had not, in fact, moved an inch since the previous day, or the day before that. His name was Kevin and he had a rather deathly expression on his rubber face. He was a scarecrow, although that's really the wrong word. Decoy would be better, or stalking horse. No, Trojan horse is more accurate.

Kevin was an idea I'd had during my last season at Redmire, but I'd not then had the opportunity to put him into 'action'. I mentioned him to Hugh before our expedition and he insisted that Kevin come too.

The plan was twofold. First Kevin stood in the shallows for three or four days with a rod in his hand. During that time the carp, which would not normally venture within a hundred yards of anyone behaving so blatantly, would gradually grow accustomed to him. Groundbait would be scattered liberally round his feet and the fish would, finally, begin to regard him as a provider of tasty things.

It was always imperative when stalking carp on the shallows that you keep down and behind cover and yet even then you could not be sure that the bait you had cast would not be snatched by a tiddler. Kevin had the advantage of being out there, standing amongst the fish. All he had to do when a big one moved towards him was lower his bait straight in front of it. The simplicity of it was positively devilish. Except, of course, that, as we all know, Kevin was a stuffed dummy.

That is where Plan B came into operation and here again I am sworn to secrecy. If I divulge too much I will spoil the film. I will, however, reveal that Plan A worked astonishingly well and that Plan B was almost staggeringly successful. Kevin now accompanies us whenever we go carp fishing.

For the first time in eight days cloud began to fill the sky. The light was too poor for film and so we all fished, all four of us. Hugh crept onto Bramble Island, where carp were bubbling close in. He had already experienced the shocking powers of a big Redmire carp. Earlier in the week he was decisively smashed up in an overhanging willow. Then he unfortunately lost two fish in the same spot, dropping his bait into the margins next to a beautiful shroud of honeysuckle. But then, on the island, his float slid purposefully away and he hooked a nice carp which, this time, did not break or shake free. I netted it for him, a bright hump-backed common of almost ten pounds. He was glad. Being at Redmire and being an angler it was intensely frustrating – bad enough to blur the lens – having to watch someone else do all the fishing. Now he had caught his Redmire carp he could once more be at ease with his Arriflex.

Bob lost a near-twenty-pounder, float-fishing on the shallows, and, as the sun reappeared again in the evening, I grassed a ten-pounder on float-fished maggots. A bigger fish rolled off the hook at dusk and then we called it a day and went off to the Royal Arms for supper.

Bob had installed himself under the old oak tree, on Greenbanks (my favourite pitch), fishing the edge of the deep water. For two days and a night he waited, and then, on the evening of the second day, his line began to run out and the birds' final chorus was interrupted by the intolerable bleeping of his bite

168

'Quite honestly', said Hugh, 'this is the best trip I've
ever been on.'

indicator. I heard him strike and saw a great upfurling of water in the centre of the pool. Shouting to Hugh to bring his gear, I raced along the bank to Bob's pitch only to find Hugh already in position, camera rolling. Bob patiently worked the carp through the worst of the weeds and it surfaced in the clear water, just beyond the bankside willows. The sun had set and the light was fading, but it was still good enough for Hugh's high-speed film. Bob was against

169

the light making a dramatic silhouette and the carp – obviously another big one – was smashing up the evening reflections and sending the ripples glinting across the pool. Leaning out across the marginal rushes, he persuaded the fish over the big net and after a moment it was lying on the grass, having its profile faithfully recorded on 16mm film. It was a common carp and we were amazed to discover that it was *another* twenty-four pounder. I immediately recognized it as a fish I had caught and returned seventeen years before. It had been my first twenty-pounder from Redmire, its lack of any pelvic fins making it a unique and unmistakable specimen.

'A brace of twenty-pounders each!' said Bob, smiling. 'Who would've believed it?'

'Everyone will *have* to believe it.' said Hugh. 'I've got it all down on celluloid.'

A blackbird and a thrush sang a final duet and then the evening fell silent. The bats appeared, wheeling round the tops of the willows, and a tangerine-coloured moon rose above the fields behind us. Hugh remarked that though he'd explored some spectacular corners of the Earth, from the Arctic to the Andes, he'd never found anywhere remotely like Redmire.

'Quite honestly,' he said, 'this is the best trip I've ever been on.'

The pool began to reflect the first stars and up in the shallows Kevin was still waiting.

CHAPTER NINETEEN

The Deepening Pool

There was a dull flash at the bottom of the river which seemed to come through the gravel, or from the gravel itself, like a discharge of aqueous lightning. The flash caught my eye as I was scanning the edge of the upstream weedbeds, looking for the big fish a friend had spotted three days before. I stared straight down into the deep water below me and after a few minutes the flash came again. It was just as if an illuminated barbel had been switched on in the dark and switched off again. A perfect profile vividly but momentarily appeared as a fish – *the* fish ? – ran its flank over the gravel and then righted itself. I continued to stare straight down, but the water was too deep and the sunlight at the wrong angle for me to discern anything other than the vague contours of the riverbed.

I wasn't standing on the bank, but perched heron-like at the top of an old willow. It hung over the deepening pool and from my position I could see across the shallows above and also downstream, where the river took a sharp left-hander to sweep away through a little copse. All around me were hay meadows, coming up bright green after their high-summer cut. The only creature along the river was a cow, standing by the bend, contemplating the water.

I glimpsed another movement at the edge of the scene I was staring at and turned to focus on it. It was the same fish, now up at the head of the pool. It filtered out of the weedbeds and spread a shadow more solid than itself across the riverbed. From above, its colouration so perfectly matched its environment that without the shadow it would have been easy to overlook. It suddenly tilted its golden flank against the sun and scalded my eyes. It had me then. I was more securely caught than any fish that was ever hooked. How big ? Not colossal. Just

173

about double figures. But it was such a majestic-looking barbel – the high back crowned by an almost sail-like dorsal, the wide span of the pectorals, the wedge-shaped head. Along that delectable stretch of river, on that morning, it didn't seem quite real. But then, no big fish seen from afar like that ever seems quite real to me. So remote and unattainable they become mythic. I had to catch this one to make it real.

I watched it for a long time as it hovered in the fastest push of water between two plumes of weed, hugging its shadow, almost invisible on the gravel. In the evening I fished for it, creeping under the tree, casting up onto the shallows and letting the lightly weighted bait come bumping down the gravel ledge and into the main pool. I had one bite, just as the sun went down. It was an eel.

Next day was cloudy and I couldn't see clearly into the pool. Nothing moved below the grey surface except the long, undulating tresses of weed. A better day for fishing, I thought, but again I only had one bite, just as the light was fading. For a moment, as something powerful chugged into the ranunculus, I thought I'd hooked my fish, but then it began to swerve about too rapidly for a big barbel. I gently coaxed a six-pounder into the net.

It rained on my next visit and the trees tossed about in the wind. I fished above, through and below the pool and this time didn't even get a bite. Then the weather was fine again, though cool. A river mist came up even before sunset. It quickly thickened and I saw a barn owl emerge from it – a mist-made bird which came wafting along the far bank and turned from white to black as it passed across the western sky. Nothing else moved until just before dark, when a big salmon leapt at the tail of the pool. The smooth water rocked, swayed and was still again. Days of rain followed and the Avon rose rapidly, lipping the top of the banks and then gushing across the meadows, filling all the overgrown, long-neglected carriers and causing havoc to the moles. Then a morning of sun and blue skies and the same the next day when I went back to the pool.

I didn't get to the river until five in the afternoon, as I'd had to photograph a violin in the sky, but the pool looked so still and seductive, while the main current boiled round the inside of the bend, that I guessed I wouldn't have long to wait to fulfil my dream. I had a strong intuition that I would catch the big fish. The spate would have pushed him down in the slacker area of the pool, where

he'd be easier to tempt.

My vantage tree and all the others round me were up to their knees in water. I hung most of my gear in the branches and sloshed to a casting position at the fringe of the half-drowned reeds. The main pool was absolutely clear of obstruction down below, but not above, where rafts of weed and assorted items of flotsam wheeled slowly round my line. Occasionally there would be an extra thrust of an undercurrent and all the flotsam would get muscled aside and swept away down the surging river. Had it not been for the weed I could almost have free-lined a chunk of Bacon Grill, but as it was I used a quarter-ounce bomb, stopped a foot from a size 8 hook. Rod and reel were the Avocet and Aerial, with 8-pound line.

Working gradually down the pool, twitching the bait gently towards me, I had a sharpish take, just as I was tweaking. I hesitated a split second, and missed.

A kingfisher streaked past, returning a few seconds later to land in the over-hanging blackthorn on my right. The sun was still warm on my right cheek, though there was only half an hour before it set, or rather slanted behind the distant wood.

I cast a little farther down the pool, inched the bait back after a few minutes and felt a slight jag. I kept everything as still as possible, being absolutely convinced that this was the moment. The pull came within a minute, nothing flashy or savage, just a slight but firm tightening. I connected and it was obviously a barbel. Was it *the* barbel? Slowly it moved left, making towards the weedbeds. It seemed indecisive to begin with, or was it merely wondering whether anything was amiss? Perhaps it thought the current had changed. Then the line cut into the packed rafts of weed alongside the reedbed and I became anxious, thinking that everything was going to clog up. However, after a moment, the fish sensibly headed out towards mid-river and the line sliced pleasingly into clear water. I added a touch of extra pressure and the barbel responded with a ferocious surge. Pressure off, the Aerial's chatter quietened almost instantly. Being only yards from the expressway of the main flow, the fish could have easily plunged in and swept off round the bend. But, fortunately, diplomacy rather than force persuaded it to stand its ground. The barbel came down the pool, then crossed in front of me, turned and slanted away again. Even with the rod completely over it felt as if it could go wherever it wished. Its movements were slow but irresistible.

Every time it made a serious bid for the main surge I tempted it back by easing off at the critical moment. After nearly ten minutes I finally managed to persuade it up and almost to the surface. But it suddenly swooped down and away, making a great bumping swirl – like a carp swirl in a still pond. It pushed deep and far, going up river and spearing into heavy weed. I stayed strangely calm, didn't overreact and waited for the pressure to ease before drawing it gradually back, with the current to help me. Yet it was another few minutes before it eventually broke surface. It wasn't easy to reach, with a great peninsula of weed in front of me and the mud going very oozy just one step out, but it came quite placidly over the net and folded just enough when I heaved everything up out of the clinging stems.

It was, of course, the one I'd been waiting for, the princely one, with its great dorsal for a crown and everything about it perfect and radiant in the late sunlight. Certainly not the biggest I've ever caught, at just under ten pounds, but definitely the best. First it had been a flash of gold, then a ghost-grey shadow; now it was palpable, real. Even when I let it go it was still more real than it had been in the beginning. But I wasn't real. I felt as light as paper as I floated back across the fields towards home.

It was, of course, the one I was after.

The sun sank behind the woods.

CHAPTER TWENTY

The Overflowing Valley

~

The Avon is a chalk stream which becomes a respectable river at Salisbury, where it is joined by
the clear waters of the Wylie and the darker brew of the
Nadder. However, today, as I write, the Avon below
Salisbury is not respectable at all. It is wild, tempestu-
ous and gigantic. It is much bigger than it was on the
day, almost a year ago, when I began this book. In fact
it is over half a mile wide in places.

It is the end of February and it has rained solidly most of the month. The
chalk downlands at the river's head and along its upper reaches, the greensand
hills along the Nadder and the sandy heathlands of the New Forest are all sat-
urated. My own well, in the chalk hills to the west, has risen over twenty feet
since Christmas. The little streams, gutters and tributaries are foaming cat-
aracts of water and the Avon is thundering over every obstacle that threatens its
headlong rush to the sea. Nothing impedes it. Its banks cannot hold it and the
river has burst over them all.

The weirpools are magnificent. The level is so high that there is hardly any
fall over the sill, just a smooth glassy curve slanting into a wide, out-spreading
explosion of spray and waves. The sound is a low, constant roar and the smell of
the spray is earthy and faintly sweet. Below the weirs, down most of the length
of the valley, the Avon's traditional course is lost amongst the flooded fields.
Last week, the first celandines and primroses were appearing along the banks;
now they are all drowned. Imagine the pressure of all that tonnage of seething
water on the actual riverbed. Not only will the silt and sand and detritus all be
swept away, the gravel and the rocks will be shifted, scoured, scooped and bull-
dozed. When the summer comes we shall have to re-map the contours and

plumb new, deeper pools.

And the fish, where are they? The salmon anglers were hoping for rain after the disastrous drought of last year, but they did not expect this. The first fish had already run up all the weirs and were in the Nadder and above Salisbury before the season had begun. And now the fishermen can't get to the river to cast. Perhaps they should be out wading the fields. Maybe the salmon are resting from the current behind molehills and down rabbit holes.

I came down here to Ibsley to see the spectacle and hundreds of acres were under water. It looked like an expansive lake, except that even over the fields the flow southwards was quite powerful. A kingfisher was sitting on a fence-post a quarter of a mile from the submerged riverbank and gulls were diving for something along the edge of a flooded hedgerow. Quite a big fish jumped in the middle of a ten-acre field. The chub will be gorged on drowned lobs, but do barbel come up off the riverbed to browse the meadows?

Just before the worst of the floods, Alonso and I went down to the Royalty. The water was just beginning to spill over into the fields and the main river was rocketing down. Fishing a favourite slack, Alonso got a barbel second cast and we ended up with six, four of them over eight pounds. We went to have a look at the Railway Pool and the bank was under two feet of rising water. The fish were gliding over the place where I usually sit and a cast to that spot produced an instant response. It was a 5 pound 9 ounce chub.

I was hoping to fish today but I couldn't get near enough to a decent slack or eddy, though I tried. I put my foot down a rat hole and got a waderful of water. The day was mild, the water temperature was in the mid-forties and, with the sudden enlargement of their home, the fish would certainly have been frisky. I am now sitting in the van, on a bit of high ground, watching the millions of gallons of water sliding down towards Ringwood. Fortunately, the church there has a high tower.

The fishing hut, where I wrote the first three chapters, will be making an impressive bow wave. I wanted to go back and finish the book there, but even if I rowed a boat to it I'd still have to write sitting on its roof. The water level won't drop for days and if I'm to keep my promise to my dear, patient publisher I must make the final full-stop tomorrow.

The river will be thundering over every obstacle on its headlong rush to the sea.

The chub will be gorged on drowned lobworms.

A five pound, nine ounce chub from a flooded river.

I would like to have at least driven across the causeway to Ibsley Bridge, but even my semi-amphibious van wouldn't survive that short journey. Bob said he might be roach fishing in the slack water behind the bridge and, if he's there, I'd like to see how he's getting on. Bob has been doing rather famously with the roach recently and has caught more two pounders than I can bear thinking about. Most of these fish were caught, incredibly, while Hugh's camera was running, during the third episode of what is turning out to be an epic film series. Yet Hugh calls it his 'pet project'. As I write he is filming wild dogs in Africa, in May he will be in the Himalayas on the trail of a snow leopard. In between these adventures Bob and I must try and catch him a big chub, a sea trout and a salmon, all in different parts of the country. Thus far everything has been as charmed as our Redmire expedition, but will our luck hold till the last cast?

The Gaffer will be pleased to see me back in time for tea and my two small children will dance about me merrily and ask whether I caught anything. They are always disappointed if I only tell them about a barbel or a roach or a chub. They are more interested if I bring home a salmon or a trout, but what they really like is a starfish.

'Are the starfish in the river yet?' asks Camilla, who is five.

'No,' I say, 'they haven't started running yet, but I might get you a seahorse.'

'Seahorses do not live in rivers,' she says, knowingly.

When Camilla was two she could, poor child, identify every British freshwater fish except the shads. She had a phenomenal memory but she also had, and has, a very good eye for detail. I took her down to the Royalty once and we went into Davis Tackle to meet Graham and Carol. It was a Saturday and the shop was crowded. While we waited for it to empty I gave Camilla a little test.

'What's that?' I asked, pointing to a stuffed pike. Easy ones first. 'But what's that?' I said, pointing to another but very poorly stuffed pike. It looked like a cross between a kipper and a fire extinguisher. But Camilla recognized the teeth.

'What's that, then?'

'Barbel,' she replied.

'And what's in this photograph?'

'Bream.'

I suddenly realized that most of the customers had stopped talking and were looking approvingly at the infant.

'I like you,' said Graham. 'You're my kind of girl. Now, what's this?'

I hoped it might be a garfish or a bloater but it was a picture of a common carp and a carp was just about the first thing Camilla ever saw. As a prize, Carol gave her a rubber sandeel, minus the hook, of course. She still has it and, naturally, it's called Carol.

Camilla got the better of me once as we leaned over a bridge at Salisbury and watched the little fishes playing in the current below.

185

It was only a tiddler which I held in my palm while he
touched it, very gently.

'They're dace,' I said.

Camilla looked harder into the water and said, 'One is a grayling.'

'I don't think so,' I said.

'Yes, I can see that big top fin.'

I moved round to get a better angle on it and she was right.

As the angling gene was once dormant in me so was the paternal instinct.
Now I am as much a doting pater as I am a passionate angler. In fact I have often
been known to pack up early just so I could get home in time to sing a lullaby
and say goodnight. Camilla has a keen eye and she also appreciates the world as
only a child can. She can tell the difference between an orchid and a columbine
or a grass-snake and an adder but she still believes in Father Christmas, dragons,
fairies and the springtime run of big Avon starfish.

Alexander is just two. Even better than starfish he likes to ride in the back-

We went dace fishing along some sparkling shallows.

pack when I'm fishing, especially when I'm wading in clear water. If I leger or roll a bait he gazes happily down at the water and becomes mesmerized by the waving tentacles of weed. He gets more interested in the fishing when I use the float; in fact his brown eyes light up just at the mention of it. He knows exactly what it means when it bobs and streaks under. He leans forward so that his face is almost next to mine and shouts 'Itty!' (he can't pronounce either 'f' or 'sh' and always rounds of his nouns with 'y').

We went dace fishing along some sparkling willow-bordered shallows last summer and Alexander was almost climbing up onto my head when I swung the first fish in. We had to wade ashore so he could inspect it properly. It was only a tiddler, which I held in my palm while he touched it, very gently, and whispered unintelligibly to it. He was transfixed and awestruck and I wondered whether I was seeing the birth of an impassioned dace hunter. I allowed him to pick it up. He cupped the little slip of silver in his hand and was still for a few moments. Without objecting, he carefully lowered it into the water when I said it was time to let him go. Now, whenever the subject of fish crops up, Alexander cups his hand and points out of the window, in the direction of the river.

CHAPTER TWENTY-ONE

The Boys on the Bridge

~

L ast summer, as I wandered along the banks of the upper Avon – not fishing, but simply enjoying the scenery – I became involved in a minor drama.

There was a little brick bridge spanning a deepish pool. Two small boys were leaning over the low parapet, staring down into the clear water. One of them was pointing, but neither spoke. So engrossed were they in whatever had caught their attention, they didn't notice me coming slowly along the overgrown bank and up onto the bridge, where I drew quietly next to them and peered down into the water.

Immediately they saw my reflection they turned sharply to face me, obviously surprised and a little shocked by my unexpected appearance. I didn't return their stare but merely continued gazing into the depths.

'Have you seen anything?' I asked.

There was a moment's pause, then, evidently reassured, one of them said, 'Just watch!'

I expected to see some gigantic trout or maybe even a salmon, but to begin with I could see nothing, just the furl of the current creasing our reflections and, deep down, a greenish cavern strewn with amber-coloured gravel and fringed with swaying weed stems. After a while I glimpsed a knife-shaped flash as a small fish flipped sideways on the bottom. Once defined it was easy to follow as it drifted and jinked in the current, finally turning and vanishing under the bridge. Was that it, I wondered, glancing sideways to see how the boys had responded? No, they were unmoved. Then their eyes opened beyond full aperture.

'There!' they hissed.

A dark-coloured fish about a foot long materialized from the shadows below

us. It moved gracefully upstream a few yards then hung in midwater, tail working slowly, pectorals barely quivering and its long dorsal like a sail in the breeze.
The two boys leant so far over the parapet, as if drawn by an irresistible power,
that I thought one of them would topple in.

'What a fish!' said one.

'What a monster!' said the other.

It was a beautiful chalkstream grayling of perfectly average size, the sort one
of the local village lads would have turned his nose up at. But these two, who
were obviously not locals, had never seen anything so astonishing in their lives.

They were, I discovered, Londoners on holiday in the area, whose knowledge
of the natural world had been mainly limited to what they had read in books or
seen on television or in the zoo. They had no experience of the life of a river, nor,
they told me, had they previously taken any interest in fish or fishing. Yet now,

A dark coloured fish materialised from the shadows below us.

because of a chance sighting, they bubbled with enthusiasm for a fish they had never heard of before, yet one that had suddenly become the most fascinating creature on earth.

Far from the bustle, mediocrity and artificiality of London, this small stream had proved the natural world to be much more interesting than they had imagined. Moreover, being real, it seemed more exciting than anything they had seen on television, because on television, they explained, you never knew whether anything was real or not.

Looking through a new, mysterious window, they had discovered the grayling. Now, for some strange reason, it seemed essential that they learn to reach through that window and make contact with what they had found. It was inevitable that the boys on the bridge would become fishermen.

I knew how they felt because something similar had happened to me at their age. My happy, normal and unfishy childhood was suddenly and completely disrupted by the sight of a seemingly miraculous fish in a village pond. It was a 'huge' golden-scaled carp and its image became indelibly fixed in my mind, invading my dreams and becoming almost god-like. So I, too, had been transformed into an angler.

The grayling eventually dropped back under the bridge and the two lads walked happily off down the lane, their heads filled with images of fish and rivers. I'd encouraged them with fishing stories, given them advice on how to begin, where to go, what to buy, what not to buy, what to expect and where to cast. I almost envied them. Whatever happened, they would probably always be dedicated, incurable anglers; long before catching anything they had been caught themselves, simply by the sight of a fish.

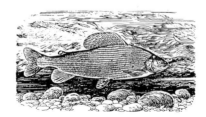